BLISS

My Pilgrimage to Santiago de Compostela

LINDA C. MAGNO

ISBN: 1463626444
ISBN-13: 9781463626440
LCCN: 2011910658

BLISS
My Pilgrimage to Santiago de Compostela

To the *little* ones in my life . . . I love you!

Acknowledgments

With a humble heart, this pilgrimage would not have been possible without the grace of God. I give thanks and praise to God for walking with me on this journey.

To my friends from Spain, Germany, Poland, Hungary, Holland, Netherlands, Ireland, England, Austria, Italy, Venezuela, Korea, and beyond, you have shared your love, kindness, and generosity to a fellow pilgrim—me. Thank you for looking out for me on the Camino.

To all the volunteers at the albergues thank you for your thoughtfulness and hospitality.

A special thanks to Ardyth Brock for editing my manuscript. Your encouragement and compassion makes writing enjoyable.

To my wonderful children, family, and friends who continue to inspire and support me in my journey in life.

Introduction

I am a pilgrim. I walked *The Camino—The Way*. My journey began in July 2007. I walked from Saint-Jean-Pied-de-Port, France to Santiago de Compostela, Spain—approximately 800 kilometers or 500 miles. This historical walk dates back to Saint James the Greater. He was the son of Zebedee and an Apostle of Jesus.

After Jesus' death, Saint James brought Christianity to Spain before the first century. Although there are many stories as to the death of Saint James on how he died, it is said that he was martyred and put into a boat and washed up on the shores on the northwest of Spain. When he was found, scallop shells were all over his body along with a staff and gourd. His shrine is at the Cathedral of Santiago de Compostela, Galicia, Spain. Today, Saint James is recognized as the patron saint of Spain and protector of pilgrims.

Every year many pilgrims from different countries around the world make their journey to Santiago de Compostela by walking the Camino. As a pilgrim, I accepted the challenge to experience the Camino on foot with my walking stick and rucksack; like many other pilgrims have done before me. This pilgrimage gave me a time to go deep within myself, and allow the spirit to flow and guide me on the journey.

During this walk, three things happened on my journey. I thought my first day would be my last day! Climbing and crossing over the Pyrenees mountain range between France and Spain, nature's four elements—wind, rain, thunder, and lightning allowed me to think I entered heaven. From my mountaintop experience, I plunged and struggled through mulch and thick wet mud up to my calves in a forest as if there was no way out of hell. The smell and taste of mud went into the depths of my pores only wanting to vomit my guts out. At that moment, I thought I had died and then came back to life again. As I looked up toward the sky, I saw tall greens trees in which I saw no end to them. All of a sudden, the tips of the trees formed a circle and I saw beautiful blue sky. I began to wail for some time. Standing in the middle of this thick mess and if I am alive, I will change my life.

Midway through my pilgrimage, once again the four forces of wind, rain, thunder, and lightning displayed itself again on the way from Boadilla del Camino to Carrión de los Condes. Only this time, lighting struck in front of me and I became blind with its power.

On the last week of my journey walking from Molinaseca to Villafranca del Bierzo, I was about to cross the street when a man rushed up to me. I stared at him thinking, "Do I know this pilgrim?" His olive green poncho, a red and white gingham shirt, khaki shorts, and hiking shoes stood out from the crowd. His shoulder length loose brown curly hair waving in the heat of day came to me and asked, "Do you speak French?" I replied nervously, "English." The interesting man said, "Be careful. Some folks were killed on this roadside last week." At that moment, I realized I needed to be vigilant on this journey. I prayed over this and connected with pilgrims as I journeyed the next several days to Santiago de Compostela.

As I met folks along the Camino, we would wish each other a *Buen Camino—Good Way!* We would ask each other, "Why are you doing this walk?" In the genesis of my walk, I wanted to experience this pilgrimage as all other walks I had already done since living in Europe. However, as I journeyed the month, a transformation developed. I rediscovered myself for whom I really am and at the same time renewed the spirit inside of me.

Buen Camino!

BLISS
My Pilgrimage to
Santiago de Compostela

TABLE OF CONTENTS

Day 1 ~ Saint-Jean-Pied-de-Port

Trust, Trust, and Trust

Here I am in Pamplona, Spain. I had a beautiful early bus ride at eight o'clock in the morning from Madrid. It is one o'clock in the afternoon and I getting off the bus. From here, how do I get to Saint-Jean-Pied-de-Port, France? The bus depot has countless buses going in and out of the station. Throngs of people are getting on and off of the buses. The weather is hot and humid. The bus terminal smelled of oil petroleum.

As I walked out of the bus station to look for a taxi, I could hear a male voice saying something in Spanish. I looked left and then right. I thought to myself; what should I do now? Once again, I heard the male voice. I looked left and there I saw him squatted down close to the ground. His hair cut clean with a hat resting on his right knee. He wore a blue T-shirt, off white shorts, sandals, and a brown backpack.

"Do you speak English?" I asked.

"Si, si. Where do you want to go?" he replied.

"To Saint-Jean-Pied-de-Port," I answered.

"I am going to Roncesvalles. It is one stop before Saint-Jean-Pied-de-Port. Do you want to share the ride?" he responded quickly and rose to his feet.

I had a moment of trepidation and I thought, "Oh my. What would my mother say to me at this moment?"

She probably would say, "I taught you not to accept rides from strangers. What are you thinking girl?"

I needed to get to Saint-Jean-Pied-de-Port. This young man would share the ride with me. Together, I would not need to spend as much money. The distance would be about a one-hour ride to Roncesvalles, and Saint-Jean-Pied-de-Port would be just around the corner. I needed to make a decision quickly.

I asked the young fellow, "Could you please ask the taxi driver how much it would cost to travel to our respective destinations?"

The young man asked my question. The taxi driver responded in Spanish. The young man interpreted, "60 euro ($98.00) for the first stop and 30 euro ($49.00) for the second stop." This is great news. I would pay just half of the fare to Roncesvalles and 30 euro the rest of the way. Immediately I looked at the young man and we nodded our heads. "Let us do it!" It made perfect sense.

The taxi driver is tall, thin, and partially bald. He has shifty eyes. I sat in the back, behind the driver. My new friend sat in the back with me. As I looked in the rear view mirror at the taxi driver, he is looking at me. He drove crazy-fast. I held onto my seat for dear life. It is a good thing that I am not alone. I am so glad that I can talk to someone in English. I began to learn trust my instincts on this pilgrimage. Five minutes before, I did not know how or when I was going to get to Saint-Jean-Pied-de-Port and now my life and destination is in the hands of strangers.

"Where are you from?" the young man asked me.

"I am from Hawaii, but currently I live and work in Germany," I replied. "And you, where are you from?" I asked.

"I am from Venezuela, but live and work in Spain. I am on holiday for two weeks, so I decided to walk the Camino. I do not know how far I will be able to progress, but I will pick up from where I leave off next holiday," he replied.

"Why are you starting to walk from Roncesvalles instead of Saint-Jean-Pied-de-Port?" I asked the young man. "I thought everyone starts from Saint-Jean-Pied-de-Port."

"The Spaniards begin from Roncesvalles because this walk begins in Spain," he replied.

"Hum, this is interesting to know," I thought. For me, learning something new in life is always exciting. Today is definitely an exciting day!

I leaned into the sharp turns, seeing green trees whirl by, and felt the bumps from the potholes along the way. Before the young Venezuelan man and I knew it, we were safely in Roncesvalles. We wished each other Buen Camino! We hugged and we kissed each other on the cheeks a fond good-bye.

I thought to myself, "He helped me to get over my first hump, and showed me I need to trust-trust-trust!" I will never see him again, but I am so grateful we met and that I trusted him.

Sitting in the taxi, I have confidence I will be able to go the short distance alone with this taxi driver, even though he continues to look at me with his shifty eyes. I focused on looking out at the scenery, noticing how beautiful the hills and landscape are as we approached France.

At last, we drive up a narrow roadway and enter the town of Saint-Jean-Pied-de-Port. I felt so relieved when we arrived. It is still daylight. I paid the taxi driver sixty euro. He smiled, grabbed me, and gave me a tight hug as if to communicate—I will never see you again! I was gasping for air by the time he let me go.

"Mucho gracias . . . Buen Camino, senora," he said.

"Mucho gracias, to you as well, senor!" I replied.

As he sped away, I waved good-bye until he was out of sight. The dust from the ground kicked up in the air as if whirling a magic spell around me. Just moments ago I was in Pamplona and now, snap, snap I am here in Saint-Jean-Pied-de-Port. Welcome Pilgrim!

Trust, Trust, and Trust

I picked up my rucksack and put my arms through the straps. I began walking up a little hill and turned the corner. As I went around the corner, there was a blue and yellow sign in multiple languages welcoming pilgrims. On the sign, there is an insignia with a staff, a cross, a bird, a scallop shell, and a drawing with cows, chains, and something that looked like another animal. This is the entrance welcoming the arrival of pilgrims. The sign reads, "Since the twelfth century when pilgrims were at their peak, thousands of pilgrims flocked to the Basque Country. Saint-Jean-Pied-de-Port is still a very busy stopping point for pilgrims on the road to Santiago; with many pilgrims of all nationalities taking refuge here every year."

As I walked through the archway, I felt my inner spirit say, "Do not be afraid. I am with you from now until the end. Enter and discover what lies ahead for you on this road."

I walked down a cobblestone roadway. I turned right and entered an aged brown and reddish brick building with an archway. This is the beginning of my pilgrimage.

An elderly man wearing a white T-shirt with a Saint James emblem on the front greets me. He speaks English and said, "Welcome, pilgrim." The gentleman had interesting dark eyes. He is bald and has a white beard. He asked me for my credential and passport.

My credential is from Germany. This is a booklet which gets stamped at places where I will stay overnight. These resting places are called albergues. I gave him my credential and passport. He looked at it and before I could say a word, I heard a "BAM"—the sound of a stamp. I looked at my credential and it read, "Accueil Saint Jacques (Welcome, Saint James), Saint-Jean-Pied-de-Port, July 22, 2007."

"When you stay overnight in an albergue, you must have your credential stamped so that the next place will know where you stayed. As you are walking, follow the blue and yellow signs. An arrow points the direction you should follow," the man said.

"Yes sir," I replied. I paid 7 euro ($11.00) for my albergue. I thanked the gentleman.

A middle-aged woman stepped forward and led me to the albergue. We walked up the cobblestone roadway. The woman took a sharp left, went into a little house, down a stairway, and walked to the end of the hall. On the left is a room—my place for tonight.

"You do know you will have blisters along the way. Do you have a needle and thread?" the woman asked.

"No," I replied.

"I will give them to someone to give it to you. You will need it for your blisters. When you have a blister, thread the needle through it, and cut both ends of the thread. Leave the thread in the blister so that .. can drain without tearing the skin," the woman said kindly.

I thanked her for sharing this helpful information. The woman shared she is from the United States and helps pilgrims with the beginning of their journey every year.

"This is something I would want to do one day, to help welcome pilgrims like myself making the walk to Santiago de Compostela," I whispered.

There are six wooden bunk beds. A lower bunk is still open so I claimed it. I admired the lovely little blue pillow, the pink sheets, and a blue and white blanket. The bed is clean and welcoming. I emptied my rucksack. I reorganized my clothes—five white T-shirts, three panties, and three sports bras. I carried a towel, a camelbak (water container) a poncho (raincoat), light sleeping bag, gloves, and a light reversible jacket with lots of pockets. I also carried toiletries, two first aid kits, safety pins, and a white cord. The safety pins and white cord are essential because after washing clothes I will need to find a tree and a place to tie my white cord and use safety pins to hang my clothes. I thought this is pretty cool.

After reorganizing my rucksack, I stepped outside to look at the scenery and landscape. I could hear the birds chirping. This is good news. There is an open area with a view of the town. The sun is bright and it is a beautiful clear day. I could hardly believe that I am truly here. The ancient wall separates this place from the town. The town is picturesque. The red rooftops on the houses, the buildings, and the church created a charming atmosphere. The trees are lush and green. Everything looks clean. The mountaintop is perfectly manicured and landscaped to perfection.

As I leaned over the wall, I noticed the town has a little eatery area and a small park-like place to relax. I quickly freshened up, and walked down the cobblestone street, then turned right, to find the eatery. I looked at the menu and pointed to the picture. I ordered paella—cooked rice in a pan with vegetables or meat. The meal is so good that I found myself savoring every bite. I am so relaxed after the meal that I found myself dozing off. I awoke when I heard music coming from the street. There is a parade put on by the townspeople. They carried flags and are wearing their cultural colors of red and green. They marched proudly passed the sightseers and pilgrims. Men, women, and children all participated in this festive parade.

After the parade, I walked around the town to explore. I found the tourist office. I bought postcards to send home to my family. I want to let them know I am here and I will begin my journey tomorrow. I have made it this far.

Trust, Trust, and Trust

As I stepped out into the walkway, I spotted walking sticks across the way. I had heard stories about these walking sticks. Word is that one needs a sturdy stick as you walk the path. The cost of these sticks varied from thirty-sixty euro. Wow, could I afford one? I struggled deciding whether to buy one or not.

Then a soft whisper inside me said, "No, not at this time. Wait, you will find a walking stick on the way. Be patient."

I walked to the place where Saint Francis of Assisi stayed when he did his pilgrimage. The building is painted white with reddish bricks and red shutters. It is well kept. It looks to be four stories. I continued walking and found the former prison cell and the local museum. It has a cluster of very old buildings made of stone and cinder block. The museum has very few windows and a beautiful arched doorway.

I found a church with beautiful stained-glass windows. There is a piece of artwork in front of the altar, perhaps done by a young person. It shows the path from Saint-Jean-Pied-de-Port to somewhere heavenly. The path shows beautiful clouds, lots of sunshine, and a beautiful rainbow. The church offers a feeling of welcome for pilgrims. The architecture of the sanctuary is three-sided and is made of the same reddish-brown cinder block tile.

I walked further along. I looked up and could see a wrought iron scalloped shell.

BLISS

My inner voice resounded, "This is it, Linda! This is your point of no return! Get ready for the big day tomorrow. Get ready for the challenge of a lifetime."

When I returned to my room, I met some folks who had settled into the other bunks. I met a couple from Germany. The other boarders are already asleep. The couple and I talked outside of our room in the little courtyard. Fortunately for me, the couple speaks English. This is the first time for each of us to walk the Camino. When I told them I am from Hawaii, but that I am living and working in Germany they were surprised, but pleased. The couple said they would only be able to do the walk for two weeks and then they must return to Germany. That is all the time they had available. We wished each other a good night's rest and a Buen Camino in the morning.

Day 2 ~ Roncesvalles

Nature's Elements

I woke early from a restful night's sleep. It must have been about five o'clock in the morning when I got out of the bunk bed. Today is my first day of this pilgrimage. I will be walking from Saint-Jean-Pied-de-Port, France to Roncesvalles, Spain about twenty-three kilometers or about fifteen miles. The highest elevation will be about 1,500 meters in altitude.

Pausing for a moment, I sat in meditation for a bit, taking deep breaths and then releasing them gently. When finished, I began to dress for my adventure. Putting on my trusty brownish-grayish shoes was a chore. The socks are extra thick to absorb lots of water. The 500 miles will be a real test for these shoes. I went to the restroom to splash water on my face and brush my teeth. I looked in the mirror.

"This is it. Today is the beginning of something brand new. What will be is yet to be experienced! I am optimistic and I need to do this for only one person. Me!" I said to myself.

As I came out of the restroom, a woman was waiting in line. We made eye contact and wished each other Buen Camino. We smiled at one another with soft laughter because we said it at the same time. I do not know who she is or where she is from.

"Does it matter? No, it does not. We are pilgrims on this road to Santiago de Compostela. Let go of any concerns and simply experience this walk," I whispered.

It is a bit cool this morning, so I made sure my light gray jacket and hat were close at hand for the trek today. I looked at my rucksack. It is all set and ready to go. Looking back at my bunk, I knew I would not see this place again, unless perhaps one day I return for another visit.

I picked up my rucksack and took one step at a time up the creaky old white wooden stairs. The smell of hot chocolate wafted in the air. It reminded me of when I was young, when my father would make hot chocolate for all six children. It was a happy thought and brought warmth to my heart and a sweet smile to my face. Lights were on in the kitchen. Other pilgrims were also gathered around the kitchen table. No one said a word. You could hear a pin drop in the stillness.

"It is true, silence is golden," I thought.

The caretaker for this albergue prepared wonderful hot chocolate to help give us the energy for the start of our journey. I drank mine and then walked over to the kitchen sink to put water in my camelbak. I am hoping this is enough water to last me the entire day. I lifted my twelve-pound rucksack up onto my back. I threaded a hose from my camelbak so that I would not need to take it out of my rucksack to drink. The caretaker came over to me and pointed to some fruits, offering me to take some along for my walk. She handed me an orange and a bread roll.

"Good Luck!" she wished me.

"Thank you. I am pretty sure I will need it," I replied with a grateful smile.

Before I left the albergue, I looked back at everyone in the kitchen, and I thought, "We will leave here today and may or may not ever see one another again. One thing we do have in common is that we are all pilgrims traveling the same distance."

Leaving the albergue, I paused to look all around me. The morning light is breaking through the night darkness. Looking toward the arched entryway to Saint-Jean-Pied-de-Port, I turned right and began my first steps of this journey. Soon, I came to a water fountain. The water in Spain is delicious! There is a scallop shell embossed on a pink tinted, upright concrete block. A faucet pierced through the shell. The drain is mossy green indicates the hoards of pilgrims that have come through here to drink from this fountain.

BLISS

Daybreak shines boldly. I came to a bridge and stopped a few moments to enjoy the water below; it is delightfully calm and peaceful. The water is glassy and still, reflecting the houses and stores lining both sides of the river. A bridge built with red cinder block tile and two arches underneath ran beyond the other side of the town. The bridge separated the town into two parts. Pink and red flowers lined a pathway leading to a restaurant bordering the river, adding charm and quaint beauty. Patio areas are small, but with inviting seating. The red rooftops of the homes explicitly spoke of an ancient beauty.

As I continued walking, I spotted the first square sign with the blue background and the yellow shell. This directs the way out of the town, leading me toward Santiago de Compostela. A few steps further I came to three black and white arrow shaped signs, two pointing right and one pointing left. One sign reads, "Chemin de Saint Jacques, Jondoni Jakobe Bidea." This sign has two pictures. One picture is of a pilgrim and the other picture has the square blue background with a yellow shell. This is it. I turned right and I am on my way.

At the turn, I see beautiful green hills and valleys. The houses are spaced long distances from each other. Farmers must live here. My nose tickled and I began to sneeze.

"This air is too fresh for me," I chuckled to myself.

I can see the cows and the goats grazing on the hillsides. The mountains and rolling hills are visible as far as I could see. The stunning beauty brought feelings of peacefulness and humility as I drank in nature's awesome beauty.

Still in a state of distracted wonder, I inadvertently stepped on something. When I looked down, there is a stick. After a double take, I confirmed for myself, yes, it is a walking stick lying in the middle of the roadway. I picked it up and held it in my left hand. The stick is a little crooked, and it stands about waist high. I test it. The stick is sturdy and perfect fit for my small frame. I could not have gotten a more perfect one, even if I had it custom made! I have heard people mention that pilgrims often do not need to buy walking sticks. They will be provided to the walker along the way.

"Yes, I have my walking stick. You will be with me throughout my journey," I shouted. I kissed it like a good friend stepped into a comfortable rhythm using my stick. I had a premonition that there will be a turning point on this journey this stick will carry me through it.

As I continued, I feel a gradual ascent. I came to a farmer and his shepherding dog directing the herd of blonde cows. He seemed to be an elderly man, wore a black hat, a green sweatshirt, and a pair of blue jeans.

He also carried a walking stick. Up ahead is a woman dressed, in a red top and black pants, leading the pack of cows. Soon she opened a gate on the hillside. The cows went through the gate one at a time into a pasture. I found it pleasing to see the cows grazing upon the rich green grass.

I stopped at Roldán Fountain for a break. While I rested, I took in my surroundings. I am extremely pleased when I saw the German couple that I had met last night walking up hill. They stopped and sat with me awhile. They shared how beautiful the countryside in Germany is, much like these gorgeous hills. We refreshed ourselves with the good clean water before we started walking again. The couple's stride is faster than mine, so they went on ahead.

"I have four weeks to finish this and I want to enjoy every single bit of it," I thought to myself.

In addition, my left knee began to pull and ache a bit, so I decided to take just my time and go my own pace. Picking up my rucksack and beloved new walking stick, I started slowly up the trail again.

When I found the next stand up concrete block with the insignia of the shell carved on it, the scallop shell had changed color, but it is still a clear marker indicating this is the path.

As I ascended to northern side of the Txangoa Mountain, it began to rain. Although the way is paved, the terrain became steep. To climb the mountain I had to switchback. The rain continued to come down harder. I stopped and reached into the very bottom of my rucksack, taking out my green poncho. Just as the poncho rested over my body, hail as big as golf balls started pummeling down. The hail bounced off of the road, back up and then down again. It is slippery and becoming treacherous.

I looked down the mountain and saw a couple walking up. They are struggling just as much as I am, putting one foot in front of the other to keep balanced. The climbing is now a struggle. My left knee is hurting a lot. The wind picks up. My poncho is flying in all directions like an untethered sail. I held onto my hat firmly. Using my walking stick, I plunged forward, through the hail and wind. It held me steady and kept me calm. My stick is becoming a true friend.

When I reached the mountaintop, the ground is hard rock. I could not see below. Again, hard winds began to blow and the rain poured down. Fog set in all around me. There is terrific thunder and lightning. It seems I am walking in the direction. Fear rises into my chest. I began to feel helpless and weak. As I begin to panic, Psalm 46:10, "Be still, and know that I am God!" filled my mind. I looked in front and back of me. There is no one in sight. Only me! I am completely alone.

"What am I doing? Am I crazy?" I said as my thoughts raced through my mind, I heard the verse again, although this time it was shorter "Be still, and know that I am!" I tried hard to concentrate. I focused on the elements of nature. I feel as if I do not keep moving I will be sucked into a vacuum and be swirled around and around with no way out. I could see no distance at this point, only step by step, one foot in front of the other.

In the midst of the wild storm, I miraculously came upon a fence with a gate open slightly. The fence is a beaten up iron. It is rusty and old. I pause a brief moment. Again, I looked forward and backward. No one is in sight.

"What do I do now? Do I go through the gate or do I stay here? Be still and know!" I muttered. That is my answer. I really have no choice, but to walk through the open gate and cross over to the other side. As I crossed over, I feel an epiphany happening. I am leaving my old self behind. As if on cue the fog lifts and the wind and the rain stops. Thunder and lightning quiets. Blue sky is above me now, as if the storm has never happened. I put my poncho into my rucksack.

"What is this? How can this be?" I asked myself. Without any other human contact on the mountaintop, I fill my soul with the bliss of the moment.

"Okay, God you are in charge here," I laughed aloud. I felt as though I died and entered heaven. I stayed a while to integrate what has just happened and to admire the beauty around me.

When I got myself together, I began a descent. I crossed a little dirt road and entered a forest. I could smell the richness of trees. They are magnificent. I recognize beech, conifers, and oak. Whoosh! In a split second, the wind, the rain, and the fog came again. I hurriedly got my poncho again and pull it over me. The flashing of the thunder and lightning are back, too. My left knee is hurting deeply now from going down the steep mountain trail. The rain pours like an open faucet in the sky. Wind is howling, causing the tall oak trees sway from side to side. I strain to see if anyone is around. Nope, there is no one but me. My trusty walking stick keeps me from slipping forward into the thick mud. By now, it is oozing up to my calves. I struggled trying to keep upright. I am petrified!

Again, Psalm 46:10, "Be still!" Good grief, I thought, "How can I be still at a time like this? I am sinking in this thick muck with nowhere to go. Nature's elements in full swing now. I need some help!"

"I am in HELL!" I groaned aloud.

I fell onto my knees, down into the thick, dark mud. Holding onto my walking stick I begin to cry aloud, "If this is Hell, I do not want any part of it. Help me, God! I need you!" Psalm 46:10 smacked me right between my eyes, "BE!" I froze still. Something indescribable from within me pulls me up. Upright, I start to walk again. Everything stops. The storm is once again gone. I could see a circle of blue sky beaming through the trees.

I am muddy from my hips down, but I do not care because I have a good feeling I feel safe and filled with a certainty and inner knowing.

A couple is walking across from me. We smiled and said, "Buen Camino." Roncesvalles is near. As I made my way through the edge of the forest and scrubs, I crossed over a little bridge. I see a graying wooden frame marked with the words: Roncesvalles. I am in Spain.

Sheep and Rocky Terrain

After crossing the Pyrenees into Roncesvalles, I found the albergue. My one-night stay is five euro. It is a large gray corrugated looking warehouse. It offers 100 beds for traveling *peregrines*, or in English, pilgrims.

I stood in line with other English-speaking travelers, waiting our turn to be called into the albergue and to find out where they will assign us for the night. A big woman dressed in a green and white flannel shirt and blue jeans shouted, "Single men on the left, single women on the right, and married couples in the middle. I will collect the money for your one-night stay and stamp your credentials. Once you get your stamp, find any open bed for the night. Departure begins at five o'clock tomorrow morning. Buen Camino."

I got my credential stamped, paid my money, and made a fast dash to the right to find an open bed. When

I got there, I found out we needed to share beds with someone for the night. I shared my bed with a young woman from Korea. We tried very hard to introduce ourselves, but found out we had a substantial language barrier. She does not speak English and I do not speak Korean. Nevertheless, we communicated with facial gestures and our hands. I had lived in Japan in the 1980's, where I learned that facial gestures and ten fingers could provide another means of communicating. It is like making do with what you have. This is all we have for now.

It is still light outside so I quickly took a shower and washed my clothes from the day. Using my safety pins and the clothesline, I hung my white T-shirt, panty, sports bra, and the bottom of my brown walking pants. Thank goodness for zipped leggings. These leggings are filthy with dried mud.

I am hungry. I ate my roll and fruit from the morning. I walked outside the albergue and saw a rock monument. It displayed some kind of fighting which had taken place probably many years ago. The plaque shows men on horses and men standing, fighting with one another. My left knee is throbbing with pain. I went back into the albergue and I asked for ice. I put it on my knee and napped on and off throughout the night.

I got up at half-past four the next morning. I felt refreshed and ready to go. My plan for today's walk will be to Larrasoaña, twenty-eight kilometers. The walk will not be too bad, I thought. It looks as if the terrain only went down, down, down. Thoughts can really be deceiving at times.

Picking up my things, I tiptoed to the restroom. After freshening up, I put on my hat and jacket. After tying my shoes, I took my clothes from the line. Some are still damp, so I pinned them to the sides of my rucksack. I thought, "Hey, the sun will dry them while I continue my journey today. Flapping clothes and underwear would not attract too much attention at this point." I am ready to go. I slung my rucksack onto my back.

Leaving so early in the morning, I did not have a chance to buy anything to eat for the day's walk. I thought maybe I would come across a place to pick up something later.

I began walking as dawn is coming upon the day. Taking a deep breath of the fresh air and lifting up my shoulders, I said, "Let today begin with sunshine and joy. After yesterday's events, what could be worst?" I passed the Roncesvalles sign and followed the yellow scallop shell pointing straight ahead. There are four people in front of me, a good sign indicating that there will be others in the back of me as well. The meadow is filled with morning dew. I could feel the freshness on my cheeks. I felt positive that today would be better than yesterday. Even my knee felt good after the night's rest.

The sun is rising. The beech wood, oak and maple trees cast tall shadows upon the field. Rolling hills are green with lush beauty and majesty, like a blanket to cover Mother Earth and to keep her warm. As the day became brighter, bundles of hay rolled up tightly and scattered strategically across the hills are revealed. Nature's beautiful simplicity is at its best. The wood fence line keeps pilgrims on their designated side and on the path.

On the way to Linzoáin, I passed an old barn. "What could this have been? Could this building have been an albergue at one time for pilgrims?" I thought to myself. The remains showed old weathered red roof tile. There are pieces of broken wood slats extending outside of the brick building. Underneath the pile of old wood slats is an entrance to the building. I wondered if I would be seeing more of these abandoned buildings along my way.

At the halfway point of my walk, I teamed up with a delightful young woman from England. She said to me, "I am doing this walk because my sister did it last year with her husband and raved about how good it would be for me to do it. My sister walked all the way to Santiago de Compostela. I can only go as far as Burgos. Then I must return back to work in England."

Sheep and Rocky Terrain

Sharing the walk this morning with a new friend is comfortable after my solitude yesterday. We came across some sheep that do not seem at all happy to see us. We could hear the sheep baaing as they watched us from a nearby hill. When turning the corner we came face to face with another group of sheep. We counted eight of them in total. They will not let us pass. They are big and wooly. Some had horns.

"Oh, oh. Are we invading their territory?" we asked aloud. We feared these sheep are either going to chase us or fight with one another. We did not want to be caught in the middle of any fighting extravaganza, so we made a fast dash out of their path. Sure enough, two sheep began to brawl. Ha, we wondered, were they fighting over a hill to determine who would become king of the mountain!

The day is getting hotter and hotter. It is only mid-morning and I am very hungry and thirsty. I drank water from my camelbak. My knee began to ache again. I could not help from limping; however my walking stick keeps me steady.

Passing the yellow scallop shell to Linozáin, we crossed a road. It was a V-shaped trek of rocky terrain, descending 400 meters straight down over the face of two mountain peaks. Beautiful woodlands along the path kept the hot sun from burning us. There is an assortment of boulders along the path. The English woman and I are hopping from rock to rock without giving it a second thought.

We heard sounds. "There must be other pilgrims behind us," I commented. Sure enough, as we looked back we saw a group of fancy-free pilgrims jumping and leaping over the rocks. We instinctively stepped to the side, moved out of their way so they could pass. Seven young pilgrims came through hastily. In a chain reaction they all called out, "Buen Camino." We replied in kind. After they gone, the English woman and I looked at each other and exclaimed, "Wow! That was a close call!" We took a couple of deep breaths, exhaled with relief, and started our walk again. From fighting rams to a leaping hullabaloo on a rocky terrain, what could happen next?

The trail is more treacherous and the growth thicker. My friend and I could not hold back our speed going down this trail. She was in front of me so I did not need to worry about her running me over.

"Is there a way out of here?" I screeched.

"Hold on. Get ready for the ride," she yelled.

We are moving just like the seven flying young pilgrims. The rocks are unpredictable and we do not know which ones are loose and would send us flying. At this point, I completely forgot about my painful knee and just kept bouncing from rock to rock.

Suddenly, I saw my friend fall. She hit her left leg and right arm rather badly on the boulders. I asked if she was all right. She answered, "My left side is fine, but my right arm is in pain. I think I may have chipped a bone in my elbow." Taking out our first aid kits and cleaned and bandaged her knee and elbow. Her elbow is already begun to swell. I gave her my stick to use until we reach Zubiri. We passed Puente de la Rabia and Zubiri is the next town. Within a very short time, we see a sign marked Zubiri.

I could feel my knee acting up again. There were, both of us hobbling along like two wounded soldiers wounded in battle and in need help. We reached the town and rested on two concrete benches. I looked up at the clock atop the church bell tower. It was almost two o'clock in the afternoon. The white concrete bell tower looks very old. The four corners of the tower are red-brown cinder blocks inlayed into a striking architecture design. There is a second tower and inside of each are two old rusted bells. As the clock hands reach the top of the hour, the bells rang twice.

While exploring around the town, I found a little market. I retrieved up my walking stick, and went into the market. I bought some dates, apples, oranges, and fresh bread. I went to see my English friend who had fallen fast asleep. On the left, I see a water fountain and filled up my camelbak. I ate the warm bread and dates. When my friend awoke she said, "I am extremely hungry and need to eat." I offered some of my newly purchased food, but she politely declined, asking for directions to the market? I pointed it out to her and she once again borrowed my walking stick and hobbled over to pick up some food for herself.

We still needed to get to Larrasoaña. It would take us another two to three hours of walking. As my English friend was returning from the market, we saw two more pilgrims walking into the town. This couple is from Holland. They sat with us, got out their lunch and we all broke bread together. It was a wonderful lunch. The young English woman was feeling better and with pep back in her voice.

"Shall we continue our adventure?" she said to me.

"Absolutely," I replied.

We invited the couple to join us. "No, but thank you," they said. "We are planning to spend the night here in Zubiri." We all wished one another Buen Camino, and off we went.

As we headed out of town, we walked passed an old house. It sat just below another beautiful hillside edged in trees. The house is made from concrete cinder block that has faded into a dull yellow and is topped with a red concrete tiled roof. Small windows speckled the sides of the house. White curtains cover the first floor windows. A white pebble walkway weaves its way to a vegetable garden in full production. I considered if this could also be an albergue for pilgrims.

Sheep and Rocky Terrain

At about five o'clock in the evening, my English friend and I finally reached Larrasoaña. We found an albergue for our overnight stay. This albergue has somewhere between fifty to seventy beds. Since we got there rather late, we were fortunate to be some of the last few to have beds to ourselves. We had our credentials stamped and paid five euro each for our nightly stay. We hugged each other with mutual gratitude and bid one another a pleasant night. An evening of simply food and sleep is fine for me. I performed my new nightly ritual of a quick shower and washing and hanging my walking clothes. I noticed I lost my sports bra along the rocky terrain today. It is no big deal though, because I have two more with me.

Ritual complete, I strolled around the small town. I came upon an old fortress and a bit further down the road, an old water fountain with a potted plant sitting next to it. The fountain stands about two feet high, bolted to the concrete slab, and it has a spout sticking out. I raised the handle of the fountain and out came icy cold fresh water. I washed my face and drank deeply.

The sun begins to set, so I walked back to the albergue. My knee is hurting badly. Once again, I asked the nightly host for ice so that I could pack my knee. They had no ice, but instead gave me a wrapped piece of frozen meat. I applied it and twenty minutes later, the soreness lessened. I returned the frozen meat and thanked them dearly.

The bunk beds are filled. I am sleeping among four men, two above me, and one on either side. There is much of snoring going on, but it is music to my ears, after the fighting sheep, the heat, and rocky terrain. I climbed into my bed and fell to sleep instantly.

Day 4 ~ Cizur Menor

Where the Bulls Run

After a restful sleep last night, I awoke noticing many hikers had already left. I performed my now usual morning routine. It pleases me how I adapt to simple and humble tasks so easily. I left a bit later, just before the albergue cutoff time. I promised myself I would take my time walking this morning. I needed to take it easy on my knee because of the stress from yesterday's rocky terrain.

Following others would be the Camino for me today. We are all headed in the same direction from Larrasoaña and onto the pilgrim's road. There is no need for me to look for yellow scallop shells. I will be a follower today. This will be good for me. It brings me perspective. My journey today is about nineteen kilometers.

As I am leaving the town, an interesting door in the front of a house caught my eye. The door is arched, brown, and made of wood. A creative black design done in metal ran vertically across the door. This unique door is framed with a yellow and gray concrete arch. A third arch of green vines is growing completely around the concrete arch. It is spectacular! There is a rectangular opening on the left side of the wooden door, adding to the architectural beauty. Four planters with cheerful pink flowers accented to the left side of the door. After a long moment of appreciation, I scurried to catch up with the pilgrims getting ahead of me.

This town has a good flat walking path. A short distance later, I came to the entrance to a beautiful vegetable garden that caught my interest. This design is also a yellow and white concrete arch. The adjoining arched gate is made from black wrought iron with two magnificent trees highlighting the entryway. Once again, I realized I am falling behind the others. "Not a time to be lost and alone," I murmured.

I could hear voices and laughter and relieved that I am not too far behind. Someone looked back, saw me, and waited. What a sweet person.

"Are you Linda from Hawaii?" a young woman asked.

"Yes," I replied.

"I have something for you from a woman back at Saint-Jean-Pied-de-Port. She asked me to bring you this needle and thread in case if you have blisters," the woman said.

I thanked her graciously. I thought fondly of the kind woman from Saint-Jean-Pied-de-Port who took the time to remember me and care about my well-being. Who would have thought to pack something as simple as a needle and thread and that they would be so important.

I could feel the heat opening my pores and beads of sweat forming. Reaching for my towel in the pouch under my rucksack, I poured some water from my camelbak and wiped my face. It was cooling and refreshing. As I looked up from the towel, I saw a river. The bordering trees are thick and strong. The sky is clear and blue. I continued to walk this path in solitude, peace, and calm. The scallop shell sign led me to cross the river.

After crossing the bridge, I came to a little town. It is quiet and peaceful. There are a few little old houses and a dirt roadway. By this time, I am hungry. I took out bread and an apple to munch on. I chose to eat and walk at the same time. I did not want to stop and take a break for fear I would fall further behind the others. On the other side of the town, the path led into another wooded area.

As the day continued, I am able to keep up with some of the others on the trail. We walked together and talked. Their first language is Spanish, but they spoke some English and with the little Spanish I knew, our conversations worked. They are cheery and interesting. There is another young woman from Korea. I asked why is she doing this walk.

"I am a Christian. I have heard that the Camino is safe for women," she replied.

"Yes, I agree with you. It is safe for men, women and children," I commented.

We walked and laughed, and shared some food together. Sharing with one another is joyful and makes our walk more enjoyable and pleasant.

I am interested in discovering some of the Spanish culture and fascinated when we came upon a hermitage in Arleta and the Trinidad de Arre Basilica.

After walking about five kilometers, I crossed over a Roman bridge. This narrow bridge has three arches and two wide horizontal portholes. After crossing the bridge and one more wooded area, the beautiful town of Pamplona in Navarra is close.

Entering Pamplona, thoughts of the city of running bulls came to mind. Joining with the others we started singing out, "Pamplona, Pamplona, Pamplona." I looked up at a clock on the face of a steeple. The church bell will be ringing in about five minutes to announce that it is half-past one in the afternoon. Pamplona is a beautiful town in the region of Navarra. I am pleased it is our resting place for lunch today. During our meal, the church bell rang three times to indicate once for the hour and twice for the half hour.

As the church bell rang, we are silent for a moment. It is a precious moment sharing silence, companionship, and food. After resting a bit, we smiled, hugged one another, and offered "Buen Camino."

Today is July 25th and it is eleven days after the ending of *encierro*, or the Running of the Bulls, which traditionally begins July 6th and ends on July 14th. I traced the way of the run from the still fresh scent of the bulls. I walked from Corralillos, where the bulls are released, down to Cuesta de Santo Domingo; through Plaza del Ayuntamiento; around Curve de Mercaderes; reaching Calle Estafeta; turning left at Curve de Telefónica; to Callejón; and, finally to Plaza de Toros, the stadium where the bullfights take place. Outside of Spain, the event is known as the Running of the Bulls and attracts fans from around the world.

In Spain, this event is called the Festival of Saint Fermin and dates back to the thirteenth or fourteenth century. Saint Fermin was from Pamplona, converted to Christianity, became a priest, and later became the first Bishop of Pamplona. He died in 303 A.D. His relics are in the church of Saint Lorenzo in Pamplona, Spain. He is the patron saint of the region.

During the walk, I imagined how it would have been with hundreds of people looking at the bulls running, folks cheering for their favorite bull or runner. The streets are narrow and stores are boarded up with thick black wood. Although the stores are protected, I could see where the bulls had left their imprints on the wood. It would take three to five minutes for the entire run. The speed is frightening.

Suddenly, my toes felt bigger than my shoes. I felt I was walking on a cushion. Using my walking stick, I made my way through Pamplona and walked through a park and onto a university campus. I crossed over a highway via a bridge and then walked into a small town called Cizur Menor.

The caretaker at the albergue is an older woman who speaks English. She explained that she is the third generation of hosts at this albergue. Her grandfather left it to her dad and now it belongs to her.

"Welcome to Pamplona Basin," the woman said cheerfully.

"Why is it called Pamplona Basin?" I asked.

"You will see why when you reach the summit at Zariquiegui tomorrow. Please keep in mind what I have mentioned to you today," she replied.

She stamped my credential, and I paid seven euro for the night stay.

I got a bunk bed near the entrance. This would keep me from disturbing anyone when I leave in the morning. Right now, I need to take care of my feet. I wondered what is going on with my feet. Why does it feel like cushions? When I took my shoes off and removed my socks, I saw blisters everywhere. They were on the outsides and in between my toes on both feet. After showering, I sat in the little courtyard and began to take care of my feet.

I took out the needle and thread from my jacket pocket. Burning the tip of the needle, I poked into one side of the blister and gently pulled the thread until it came out of the other side. As instructed, I left the black thread inside the blister and cut the ends off, leaving some thread hanging loosely. This would allow the thread to absorb and release the water from the blister. I had six huge blisters, two on my right foot and four on my left foot. After nursing my feet, I walked with the aid of my stick to see the hostess of the albergue. I asked her for an ice pack for my sore knee.

"I see it is not only your knee. You have some mighty blisters as well," she said with a smile.

"I feel rather wounded tonight. I hope I can continue my walk," I confided.

She smiled with compassion and nodded knowingly. When I reached my bunk, I applied the ice pack to my knee and quickly fell asleep.

After a nap, I got up and noticed that my blisters were flattened. I did not remove the thread from the blisters yet. Slipping on my walking shoes, I returned the ice pack to the generous woman. I thanked her graciously and went outside to find a market to buy some food for my supper and for the upcoming summit adventure. I found a little market and picked up some bread rolls and oranges. I must say living on bread, water, and a bit of fruit fills me up quickly these days.

As I was returning to the albergue, I saw an old building with Roman architecture. It was a hospital for pilgrims in ancient times. A red and white flag is flying above the roof. From a distance, it looks like a miniature castle. The design shows several different dimensions of the concrete and small windows. Like most of the buildings I have seen on my trip, the doorway is arched and boasted three columns at the entry. Covered circular windows are on the side of the structure and are shaped liked six-petal white flowers. When I turned, I saw a church.

The church has a tower with two bells. There are two arches leading into the entrance of the church. To explore it, I would have to climb at least thirty steps. Taking each step carefully, I successfully reached the top. I walked over to the edge and I could see a panoramic view of rolling hills and mountains. It is obvious that I had left the magnificent city of Pamplona. Here it is all farmland.

As I entered the church, townspeople are sitting in prayer. I heard the bells ring six times, announcing it is

six o'clock in the evening. I attended the liturgy celebration even though it was said in Spanish. This church
is simple and beautiful. Flowerpots sat upon pedestals,
lining the back wall. A stained-glass window, a crucifix,
a small altar with a white cloth over it, one candle, and
the Book of the Word in front of the altar placed on a
small stand made up the decor of this humble place of
worship.

As I sat quietly, I recalled today is the Feast Day of
Saint James. He is the patron saint of Spain. It is written
in the Bible that Saint James was the son of Zebedee.
He was a fisherman in Galilee. It is told that as an
apostle, Saint James found his way to Spain to spread
Christianity. In 44 A.D., Saint James was martyred. I
found it incredibly moving to be here on his feast day.

After Mass, I walked back down the thirty steps
and cautiously made my way back to the albergue. I
see many folks I walked with today. They, too, will be
spending the night here. Many have blisters, so I vol-
unteered to help those who needed assistance. Little
whimpers of pain could be heard now and then. When
all were doctored, a meal, and laughter cheered us all.
Getting to sleep tonight is not a problem for anyone.

Day 5 ~ Puente la Reina

Mountaintop Experience

Early this morning I depart from Cizur Menor. I am looking forward climbing to the summit of Zariquiegui. As I begin my walk, my blisters are not bothering me as much as yesterday. My feet and knees are very important at this time. My walking stick, hat, shoes, camelbak, and rucksack are essentials for this journey.

Today I will be ascending an additional 250 meters in altitude. It is a clear and hot day. The burning heat of the sun is making me sweat like a leaking faucet. I wipe myself with a wet cloth to keep cool. I put the cloth around my neck.

Climbing the slope, I see huge beautiful sunflowers. The center of the sunflower is bigger than my face. They are beaming yellow. They stand tall and strong. I see acres and acres of these sunflowers. They bring splendor and beauty to the hillside. I stop and turn around. I see that I am leaving behind Pamplona and the Pyrenees. Something came over me.

I started asking myself questions, "Why am I doing this walk? Is it for the experience? Is it for the sake of just doing it?" I am fifty-seven years old. I desire to do this walk. I have been carrying a heavy baggage these last couple of years. After being married for many years, I am now divorced and single. In 2003, I left behind my family and friends and came to Europe to work. The honest truth is that I came to Europe to heal. The job opportunity is my saving grace.

Here it is 2007 and I am still carrying this burden, holding onto something that I need to let go. The ending of my marriage nearly destroyed me. "When am I going to let go and begin to live again? It is time to move on and rediscover life once more," I shouted.

Just before coming to Europe in 2003, I learned of this pilgrimage. I knew it would be safe for me to do. Deep inside of myself, I could not wait any longer to do this walk. I did not want to put it off until after my retirement one day. I needed to let go and detach myself from what I have been holding onto these past years. In less than nine months, I will be moving back to Hawaii. I will be reunited with my family and friends again. Time does heal a broken heart and now it is to begin anew.

Back at the foothill of Zariquiegui, tears begin to stream down my face. I cannot control myself. I feel as if a dam is about to burst. Now that my sadness has begun to release I cannot stop it.

"Why is this happening to me?" I asked.

"I will help you through this. Do not be afraid. Let go," my internal voice whispered.

"Help me. Please take my hand. I cannot do this alone. Lift this burden from me," I begged. Then I recited a beautiful scripture. Psalm 51:10, "Create in me a clean heart, O God." Repeating this passage over and over, I hang my head and walk. After a long while, my tears stop.

By now, the sun feels extremely hot. Three others pass me and nodded, "Buen Camino." I wished them the same. Something tugs at me from within me, "Walk, walk, walk. I will be your strength," is the message.

As I reach the summit, I look around and see a beautiful range of mountains. There it is Pamplona Basin. I feel a broad smile cross my face and I sigh with relief. Pamplona sits at the basin. These mountains form a circle. Magnificent beauty surrounds the area. Looking as far as I could see, I left behind Pamplona and the Pyrenees.

I lifted my shoulders and took three deep breaths. Without any hesitation, I left behind my old self. This is the moment where I begin anew. I thank the spirit inside of me for giving me the strength I thought I lacked when I feel weak.

When I reach the summit, I come upon a group of seven folks having a little break. The group sat leaning against a stonewall. One of them waved to me, calling out, "Senora." She motions me to join them. All but one female was speaking Spanish. The English-speaking woman gave me an orange. I thanked her. The whiff of the orange caused my taste buds to explode. It smelled so refreshing. The orange was cold. I ate each slice slowly and with special delight. Once again, I thanked and wished each of them a Buen Camino. They smiled and repeated the same.

Looking over to my right, I see some curious human-size statuary. The figures are of men, women, children, and a dog. They are made of rusted metal. One of the figures sat on a donkey; two others straddled horses. They look like pilgrims crossing over the summit in a single file. Looking closely, I see they are a mixture of different generations. Some are from earlier times. They are wearing three-cornered hats and were dressed in coats down to their knees. I found this beautiful artwork welcoming me as I stand on the mountaintop.

Here I am at the peak of Zariquiegui. I see a yellow arrow in front of me leading me on. It is time to continue my journey. I begin to descend to Uterga and Obanos. At this point, I am halfway to Puente la Reina.

As I begin to walk downhill, the terrain becomes rocky. I cannot help but go fast even though it is not my intention. Already it is midday and the sun is making it hot. In front of me, I spot a man walking slowly. The steep pitch of the trail made it difficult to slow down. I could not stop myself, but I did not want to run into him. I wove over to the right side to prevent an accident. I tried to catch myself from falling.

"Excuse me. Excuse me," I shouted.

"Si, si, senora," he replied.

"Whoa! I think I am going to fall!" I screamed. My stick flew in front of me. I felt something grab my left arm and pull me back quickly.

"Mucho gracias, senor," I said with glee.

"Are you okay?" he asked in laughter.

"Yes! Thank you so much for saving me! I thought surely I was going to injure myself on these rocks," I shook with relief.

"Why are you walking so slowly?" I asked him.

"I have many blisters. I am walking in much pain," he replied.

"I am sorry for you. Yes, blisters can be very painful," I commiserated.

"Where are you stopping today?" I asked.

"Puente la Reina," he answered.

"Is it all right if I walk with you? I will be stopping there also," I said. I tracked down my walking stick and resumed my walk with a new friend.

As we came into the village of Puente la Reina, I thanked this pleasant man for sharing the walk with me. We hugged and wished one another a Buen Camino. I checked into the albergue and went back outside to enjoy some afternoon time and relax. There is a beautiful grassy area outside the albergue. I ate my leftovers and rested for a little while. Reflecting on the day's walk, I filled my lungs with a deep sigh of relief.

"There is a reason in life for everything. I need to stop, look, and listen much more," I coached myself. I felt I had accomplished something today.

Some of the other pilgrims are gathering on the grass. Four of the townspeople came to join us. One of them announced, "After your long walk today, we have come to give everyone lessons in foot massage. We will teach you how it is done then if you would like, you may massage each other's legs and feet." How great this is, I thought to myself.

A woman started on my legs and feet. I felt so relaxed I wanted to fall asleep. I did not want her to stop. The woman's touch was strong, but gentle. It seemed that she was removing every lump and bump I had. Then we were directed to switch. I began to massage the woman's legs and feet. The massage was healing. It released many of the aches, pain, and tightness.

After the massaging was finished, we sat around chatting about our walk. I looked to the side and saw clothes drying. Eventually, I got up and went to do my laundry. I found a little space for hanging my clothes. There was a nice breeze blowing so it would take no time at all for the clothes to dry. The shade on the grass had widened. Lying down in the plush green seemed an ultimate dream. I felt the cool of the day wrap me in deep comfort. I dozed off to dreamland.

When I awoke, there was still a bit of sunlight. I put on my jacket and hat and went for a walk through the town. I found a market and bought some food for tomorrow's journey. I met a woman from Italy. We walked together down a narrow street and came to a medieval bridge. It had large beautiful arches. The water under the bridge was so still that it reflected a mirror image of the bridge. Calmness and quietness was serene. Once we crossed the bridge, we looked for our departure route for tomorrow morning. We found the yellow scallop shell beckoning to us. I am so happy to know I am not the only one planning ahead for the next day.

Back at the albergue, I could smell the aroma of something wonderful cooking. I went directly to the kitchen. There I saw the same group of folks that I had met earlier during the day up at the summit gathered at the dinner table. The generous woman who had given me the orange stood up and called me over to sit next to her.

"Hola. Linda, please come and join us for dinner," she said.

I made my way to the table and sat next to her. It has been almost a week since I have eaten a good meal. "Wow, this is great!" I rejoiced. Eating pasta, salad, bread, and dessert filled my appetite.

The kind woman introduced me to everyone. They were a spiritual group on this pilgrimage. Their spiritual director was a priest. I felt truly welcomed. We prayed and broke bread together. We shared our tales of the day's events. Laughter and joy filled the room. We could also see and empathize with each other's pain; even still, tonight we come together and celebrate. Tomorrow is not here yet. We simply have now. This is all that seems to matter. As the evening came to a close, I thanked them for their warm hospitality.

Many were asleep by now so I quietly tiptoed to my bunk. Reflecting back on today, I pondered upon my experience with my breakthrough. My baggage has been left behind somewhere at the top of the summit floating out into the cosmos. The tears I shed today were of sadness, but one day there will be tears of joy and gladness again. I am reminded, "Create in me a clean heart, O God." I am not alone on this walk. I need not be afraid.

Day 6 ~ Estella

Light and Hope

Leaving the albergue early in the morning, the temperature was on a rise. Today is going to be another hot day.

As I was walking and crossing over the medieval bridge in Puente la Reina, I turned right, touched, and waved good-bye to the yellow scallop shell. Today's distance will be about nineteen kilometers to the town of Estella. I will walk through four towns—Mañeru, Cirauqui, Lorca, and Villatuerta before reaching my destination.

I feel good today. My trusty rucksack is beginning to seem weightless on my shoulders and back. It now helps to keep me balanced. The pain in my left knee is throbbing less. Here I am almost one week into my journey and I am beginning to feel lighter. I noticed my walking stick is beginning to get shorter. As I hold it in my left hand, the stick pulls me forward as I crouch over. What is happening here? Is my stick walking me or I am walking my stick? If I am walking my stick, this is not the time to be pulling muscles, especially in my back. Needing all the strength I could get during this time in my life is important to me.

"What is important in life for me at this moment in time?" I asked myself. Many things run through my mind, but the word hope hits me. Hope keeps me going each day. I hope to complete this walk. The Basque region of Spain offers hope. Many others have walked this way before me and many more will come after me. The hope is in the taking of one step at a time and feeling the earth below. It gives me the drive to continue, and ultimately complete the Camino.

Zigzag trails carve out a perfect path. From a distance, I think I see a village on the hillside. Different colors of yellow, red, white, and tan sprinkle the rooftops that encircle this town. "Am I imagining all of this? It is so hot. Maybe it is a mirage! Why does it have to be so damn hot?" I yelled aloud. "My knee is in awful pain. The blisters are slopping and swishing inside of my wet socks. HELP me!" I pleaded. I hung my head and began swaying from side to side.

Impulsively I stood up straight and tall. I thought to myself, what if someone behind me sees me staggering like this! What if they heard me shouting and yelling? They would likely think I am drunk out here in the middle of nowhere. I could be asked to leave the

Camino, not what I want to do right now. "Do you want to end this?" I questioned myself. "Get a hold of yourself you fool, and finish what you have started. Linda, be strong," I coached myself. "I am not quitting! I will not quit!" I declared. And then, I sobbed.

Approaching a town, I see an orchard of green grapes covering the side of a hill. The grapes looked fully ripe and ready to be picked. As much as I want to pull a grape from its cluster, I willed myself not to do so. Instead, I stare at the grapes and imagined one in my mouth, bursting with juicy sweetness. Four bunches of rich grapes filled just one vine. Healthy green leaves give shade to the grapes. One day they will all become wine. Getting into my camelbak, I drink my tasty water.

On my left, I see dry grass along the path. Something caught my eye. Four distinct structures made of yellow rocks. The rocks are different shapes and sizes, clusters on a little hill. Could these rocks be a directional sign? What direction did they indicate: north, south, east, or west? I wondered. As I passed the rocks, I pondered if they represent something, perhaps beyond my imagination.

As I passed the vineyard, I felt hungry. I needed something to eat, so I stopped. I pulled out my dried dates and the slightly stale bread from yesterday I had just finished eating heartily when I saw a group walking the trail. I heard someone say, "Hello, Linda." I squinted hard. I recognized them as the same group I met yesterday. It is so nice to see familiar faces. We sat together while they had lunch.

After a pleasant conversation and a bit of a rest, we got up and started walking. I could not keep up with this group so I strolled behind them. In a short time, they were out of my sight. Hearing their laughter, I knew they were not too far ahead.

The road became narrow. I could see three others standing and talking. As I got closer, I saw I needed to cross a narrow wooden bridge. Before the bridge, on the left side there was an ancient rock wall. It looked as if at one time it was part of the bridge itself. I approached the bridge and thought NO WAY. I could not get to the other side on this rickety old thing. Suddenly my right foot broke through one of the wooden boards.

"Help! Help me," I bellowed aloud.

One of the nearby travelers heard my cries, and ran over and pulled me up. He spoke in Spanish.

"Mucho gracias, senor," I said with much gratitude. My leg was bleeding and splinters of wood had pierced my skin. The resourceful young man immediately began applying pressure quickly to stop the bleeding. Once the bleeding stopped, he washed my leg with water and wrapped it in a makeshift bandage. I could not thank him enough.

He smiled and said, "Okay?"

Light and Hope

I returned his smile knowing that because of his help I would be fine. I waited a little while before walking again. Letting go of the mini-trauma with a deep sigh, I retrieved my stick and began putting one foot in front of the other once again.

After crossing a roadway, the path dictated that I needed to go under an archway. It looked strange at first. Being alone, I became a little hesitant. Still babying my leg, I carefully wobbled down a few steps and turned left, I saw two arches. The exceptional beauty of the scene stopped me in my tracks. Thick green woodlands and hills captivated me. Having just left rough terrain to come to this parallel lush land is simply incredible. The sunlight shining between the arches created such a glorious sight that I stood there drinking in the blissful moment, not wanting to walk away.

I began to feel lighter and a rich sense of hope filled my heart. Slowly edging forward, I felt as if I was walking on air. I confirmed that I will not give up now. Yes, I may have a slight injury, but I will continue nonetheless. Finishing this walk is what is important.

Upon reaching Villatuerta, I am only three kilometers from Estella. Walking into a church, a short elderly woman wearing a light blue blouse and blue pants is busy stamping everyone's credentials. As she stamped mine, I thought how many of these have this woman stamped. How many folks has she met for but a moment, all on their vision quest, each taking a personal journey? Watching her stamp and write July 27th into my book gave me a good feeling, knowing that I have made it this far and now clear about making it to the finish. I took my credential and sat in the church for a little while in rest and light prayer.

When I finished my meditation, I took my stick and walked outside. Looking around, I closed my eyes and deeply breathed in the fresh air. Walking passed orchards picked up my spirit. I could hear water coming from somewhere. I soon saw a river. I came to a hermitage, then to a narrow bridge, which I crossed into Estella.

I stayed at an albergue in Estella and paid seven euro for the night. After checking in, I asked the caretaker to look at my injured leg. He removed the wrappings and applied a medicinal cream. The cool cream calmed the ache. I thanked him and made my way to the restroom to freshen up. It is three o'clock in the afternoon. I looked at my bunk bed and thought, siesta time.

After my nap, I made my way to the market. While I was picking my necessities for tomorrow, I met a woman from Italy. We walked back to the albergue together. We dropped off our new purchases and then went back out. We found St. Peter's Church. It seemed to be a Roman design with a tall steeple and bell tower that towered over the town. The ancient church sat high upon a hill boasting many steps leading to the arched nave. We took it slow as we walked up the steps and into the church. A Mass is about to begin, so we stayed for the celebration. After Mass, I walked out to the back of the church and found the ruins of a cloister. I spent a long while contemplating the ruins, imagining the history.

As I walked back into the church, I spotted my new friend still sitting quietly in prayer. The choir is rehearsing. I sat in one of the pews and listened to the angelic voices. After my episodes of this day, the music helped to shed some light as I closed my eyes and reflected how beautiful life is, including the ups and downs.

My friend came over to me and asked if I was ready to go back to the albergue.

"Yes, I am about ready to go. The music is beautiful," I responded.

She nodded in agreement. As we were walking back, we were mostly quiet.

"What was the priest saying in the Mass? I could not understand him," I asked.

"The priest said simply we need to understand the Word," she explained.

I chose not to say anything more. Tonight it seemed appropriate to be quiet. Breathe in, absorb everything, and peacefully wait for tomorrow.

BLISS

Crawling into my bunk, I got myself comfortable. Although I feel some aches and pain, I accept that this is life. I may stumble and fall, but it is getting up and trying again; moving forward that will help to make me a better person. I will heal and be stronger every day on this pilgrimage.

Today, I saw beauty and experienced pain. In this same day, I experienced the comfort of someone coming to help me. I may not see this person again, yet I will remember the kindness and the light and hope I experienced today. The joy this brings to me words cannot begin to describe.

There is something more to this Camino than just a walk. It brings people from all over the world and many walks of life together. As I begin to fall asleep, the stillness of the night settles upon everyone here. As we sleep in silence, the pain in my body also subsides. We are connected for now and will begin anew tomorrow. For now, there is light and hope. For me, the fruit from this is joy.

Day 7 ~ Los Arcos

Letting Go

I got up this morning feeling sticky because it was muggy. Unzipping my pant leggings, I felt a little more comfortable. When the beaming sun becomes hot today, I hope to be somewhere in the shade. It is almost a week since I began this walk. My pants are becoming loose and baggy. I fastened a safety pin to the right side of my pants to keep them from falling off when I walk. Although I do not mind losing weight, I think this may be too much too fast because I will need a great deal of stamina in order to finish walking the Camino.

After walking two kilometers, the path split. My choices are to either go through Ayegui or walk pass Irache. While I was walking with some fellow travelers today, we decided to take the route to Irache. We came to Bodegas Irache. There we were able to refresh ourselves from two fountains. One offers water and the other wine. This will help to give us the energy we need to reach Los Arcos today. I refilled my camelbak with water. I then tasted the wine. It is delicious! I am so glad I decided to go this way. It is really fun and rewarding.

Upon leaving Irache, I walked alone for a spell. I came to a grove of trees that provide a welcoming shade. I imagined being a bird flying from one branch to another among the trees. My arms felt as light as feathers. Flapping my wings, I imagined being lifted higher and higher. As I continued soaring up into the sky, I could see the magnificence of God's creation below. How marvelous this is from above. I felt as if I could fly. There is nothing to bother or to stop me. I felt as though I could do this all day. Eventually I came back to my mission of walking the Camino and left behind my imaginary flights.

As I approached the town of Villamayor de Monjardín, the panoramic view of this tiny clustered village resting among rolling hills captivated me. A church stood tall, as if peering above all of the buildings. Making my way into the town, I passed by a vineyard. The smell of the grapes filled my nostrils with their sweet aroma. It is delightful.

In town, I met up with a group of friends. They were having lunch in the shade of umbrellas in the center of a courtyard.

"I think that perhaps your walking stick may be too short. It seems quite worn down. If you keep using it the whole way you are going to be walking crookedly by the end of this journey," one of the men in the group commented.

"This stick has been with me from the beginning. It is now a part of me. I have walked more than 107 kilometers with it. I have become attached to it," I said in hopefulness.

"Si, senora. However, if you continue to walk in this fashion you will end with a back problem. Please, take my stick. It is much taller and sturdier," the gentleman said convincingly.

"I do not want to give it up yet. I will need to think about this," I answered.

"I will not walk all the way to Santiago de Compostela. You may have mine, when I leave my journey on the Camino," he offered.

I did not say anything, but nodded in appreciation. Even with his generous offer, I continued to embrace my stick. He looked at me and smiled knowingly I need to switch my walking stick.

As we had our lunch and shared food, the same gentleman walked directly up to me. He put his walking stick in front of me. "Please, take my walking stick senora and give me yours," he insisted.

I handed my stick to him and graciously received his. Tears rolled down my face. I was parting with something I had carried with me from my beginning in Saint-Jean-Pied-de-Port. The separation was like saying good-bye to a trusted friend. I stood and faced my new wise and considerate companion.

"Mucho gracias," I said with deep appreciation.

He hugged me kindly. I told him that I will always remember him and our exchange. With that, we parted, wishing one another a Buen Camino.

Soon afterward, I left the group and headed onward going solo. I need to become acquainted with a new friend, my walking stick. It is at least four feet tall. This stick is much taller than my old one. There are bumps on it, however it has a nice curve to it and it feels sturdy. The top of the stick is shaved, making a grip for my hand to hold. The rest of my walk today is strictly descent. It will be manageable.

Without transition, the greenery and shade dis-appears abruptly. I am in a desert now. Water began to secrete from my pours and began to run down my entire body. Then the heat of the sun seemed to explode. I began to feel as though I could not do this much longer.

"It is too hot!" I shouted aloud, venting my discom-fort out into the desert. Even though I have spent most of my life in Hawaii, in the tropical climate, I have never been so hot in my life. I wondered if this heat is ever going to subside. There is no one in sight. I am alone along this narrow trail, edged with small stonewalls. I cannot find the yellow scalloped shell that I count upon

Letting Go

to direct me. The only thing I see is the restrictive pathway that I use to keep me on track. I am baking in this heat. My hat is soaking with sweat and my head feels heavy with pressure. I can feel my body dragging as I walk. I got out my hand towel, wet it with water from my camelbak, and put it around my neck. Coolness began to soothe my overheated body. I began feeling refreshed. I spontaneously began reciting Psalm 23:

> The Lord is my shepherd, I shall not want.
>   He makes me lie down in green pastures;
>   he leads me beside still waters;
>   he restores my soul.
>   He leads me in right paths
>   for his name's sake.

> Even though I walk through the darkest valley,
>   I fear no evil; for you are with me;
>   your rod and your staff—they comfort me.

> You prepare a table before me in the presence
>   of my enemies; you anoint my head with oil;
>   my cup overflows.

> Surely goodness and mercy shall follow me
>   all the days of my life, and I shall dwell in
>   house of the Lord my whole life long.

By this time, I am walking in a dark valley. Everything around me seems gloomy. I know that I am not alone because God is with me and God will not forsake me.

"What must I do to make it right in my life?" I questioned myself. "I am trying," I wept in tears. My weeping became uncontrollable. I began to hear a voice whispering, "I am with you always." I stopped and waited, hoping I might hear more. I closed my eyes and took a deep breath.

"Yes, Lord you are with me. Please take my hand. Please be the footprints in the sand. I cannot do this without you. I need your help," I said in discomfort. After more deep breathing, at last I began to walk again.

Crossing over ravines along the countryside made it difficult to walk. I thought my new walking stick is carrying me through this heat wave. I could feel myself stumbling. Tripping over rocks today would not be a good idea, I cautioned myself. Mindfully, I began placing one foot in front of the other. I held onto my walking stick tightly.

"Hold me straight up. If I should slip, catch my fall," I prayed. I am in agony. Using my towel, I wiped my face.

By early afternoon, I was nearly crawling into Los Arcos. I saw a few of the folks I knew. They came over and asked, "Are you okay? Do you need help?"

"No, thank you. I need to rest then take a cool bath," I answered in distress.

They pointed in the direction of the albergue. It is not too far from where I am standing. Then I walked to the albergue. After getting my credential stamped and paying four euro, I walked to find my bunk for the night. Plopping my rucksack down, I covered my face and breathed deeply in sheer gratitude, "I made it. I am here," I sighed with inner joy.

Once at the washing area, I could feel pains in the back of my legs. I turned to look. I saw bright red sunburn over the length of my legs.

"Great! This is all I need. The backs of my legs are burnt and blistering! I do not deserve this!" I cried out in pain. Removing my leggings this morning was not a good idea. I asked someone to look at my legs.

When she took a look, the woman said, "Oh my, you have serious sunburn." She bent over to look closely and remarked, "You have blisters, too."

I could feel my shoulders drop. My arms sagged downward. "What do I do now?" I asked in despair.

I made my way to see the caretaker of the albergue. I showed him my legs. He touched the sunburn. I jumped back and screamed, "OUCH!"

"I have medicine for you," he offered in kindness. After he applied the medication, he stood up and smiled at me with commiseration and reassurance in his eyes.

"Mucho gracias, senor," I responded, feeling miserable. I am in trouble now. Pain! This is going to add a new level of hardship to my journey.

"Senora, do not take your leggings off!" he strongly cautioned.

"Yes sir," I replied, having learned my lesson. Then I got some ice for my knee and slowly wabbled to my bunk. My bunk looked like a soft pillow. I sat gingerly, babying my burns. I rested my head on my rucksack and fell asleep.

I stirred from my nap as the smell of food made its way into my nostrils. What is this? I could feel someone touching me. Opening my eyes, I could see a woman standing before me.

"Linda, come join us. We have made supper. Come eat some pasta with us," she said.

"Thank you. That sounds wonderful! I am out of energy. Would you please help to pull me up? I can barely lift myself," I groaned as the woman helped me sit up.

She then helped me walk over to the dining area. I could see my friends sitting around the table. They waited until I sat down. We blessed the meal, each in our own language. Someone handed me a piece of bread. I ate my meal in small bits. The nourishment brought me great delight. I have never realized until now just how good food could taste.

Letting Go

A nice gentleman offered me a glass of wine. I declined his offer. He looked at me with disappointment. "Thank you for your kindness, but I cannot drink this glass of wine. Today the walk has given me great pain and discomfort," I said.

He smiled. I could see from the look on his face that at some time along his way, he had shared a similar pain.

Eating with friends is an enjoyment. Although we may not know each other's languages well enough to carry on a full conversation, the comfort of our warm company and sharing a meal together brings down any personal barriers and separatism. There is something special and universal about food that brings people together.

One of our friends left the table. He came back with an old leathery bag. To our delight, he took out a flute. As he played, the music gently filled the room. He played with grace and charm. The angelic music set the mood for a deep rest tonight. In contrast of walking such rough terrain today, sweet harmony embraced the group. We sat in quiet contentment.

Unexpectedly, I saw the gentleman who had given me his walking stick. He came up to me and smiled, "I am glad to see you."

"Thank you for giving me your walking stick. It has brought me to Los Arcos. I may not have made it today if I had used my old stick," I said in gratitude.

Surrendering my walking stick today, helped me realized letting go is not always so terrible after all. The hard part is knowing when to let go. I may not see what is good for me, but at times others may be able to see what I cannot. I am trying to allow myself to be open and let in the wisdom of others who see what I do not. Accepting this man's wisdom has offered me a chance to be trusting.

Filled with thoughts of gratitude and feeling connected to the hearts of such kind people helped to ease the pain of my sunburn. It is not causing nearly as much discomfort now. The swelling has gone down. I am now confident that the blisters will heal and my legs will be strong once more. Every day there is a new opportunity for learning and processing along this journey. I am feeling much stronger to face up to new and unexpected things now.

Feeling peaceful and fulfilled, each of us made our way to our respective bunk for a much needed night's sleep.

Day 8 ~ Logroño

Stay with Me

I began my walk today with a friend from Italy. This week I am learning that walking with someone early in the morning is helpful for me. Leaving Los Arcos behind, we walked through a dark wooded area. Step by step we made crackling sounds in the woods. Over time, we began to hum to the rhythm surrounding us. We saw the sky turn from darkness into light. As sunbeams brought daylight to the sky, we beheld an incredible sunrise. A fan of dark yellow ribbon burst upward, giving rise to the sun. The beauty stopped me in my tracks. I was mesmerized by the magnificence before me. This sunrise splendor set the tone for our journey ahead.

"What is in store for me today? What lessons might I learn? Will I make it? How hot will it be? When will I get to Logroño?" I wondered.

After a while, I grounded myself and began walking forward. I could see my friend in a distance. Calling out to her, she turned and waved to me. Her message seemed to say: "I will see you later."

Urgently, I began having stomach cramps. I needed to find a place quickly in which to relieve myself. I found a tree and ran. I relieved myself and rested for a bit. Wow, that was close! Feeling better and chuckling to myself, I realized that even something as basic as my bodily functions are part of my journey. I got up and resumed trekking.

By this time, the heat from the sun was also rising. I have learned that I can eat and walk at the same time without needing to take breaks. My walk today will be twenty-seven kilometers to Logroño. It will be manageable. The highest point today will be Nuestra Señora del Poyo. Walking over a bridge, I crossed the San Pedro River. A few kilometers later, I came to the village of Sansol and rested. I sat down on a tree stump. I reached into my jacket and pulled out an orange. I peeled it with great care and respect because I knew that I needed to savor the juices for nourishment. Each slice I bit into burst with sweetness. The taste was so heightened it was as if I had never eaten an orange before. This refreshment gave me the energy to continue my walk.

As I strolled along, I began thinking about my family back home in Hawaii. Until today, I did not realize how much I missed them. Feelings arose within me.

Stay with Me

Tears began to stream down my face like a flowing river. I held my walking stick close to me.

"What is happening to me? Why am I crying like a baby? Can I continue today?" I asked myself.

My thoughts became clearer. I have buried deep down inside of myself the hurt and pain I have experienced in my life. Through my ways and actions, I have caused pain to those closest to me: my children, my family, and my friends, without realizing until now the damage that I may have done. On the heels of my tears, I also became acutely aware that I needed to forgive those who have hurt me as well. I began to pray fervently.

"I am humbly sorry for all the wrong I have done to others. I also forgive those who have injured me. What have I done? Help me get through this and move forward, Lord. I am in this valley of tears and I am hurting inside and outside. Transform me to make changes in my life," I pleaded in despair.

I called the name of each person and begged for forgiveness. I cried out each name and most humbly began to forgive each person who had hurt me.

Not seeing another person around, and feeling safe in my solitude, I let myself moan and groan aloud like someone who has been physically attacked. With each sound I released, I kept focused and prayed for that person.

"I am not a bad person. Stay with me now and always. I need help. Please make me a better person. I am truly sorry. I have to change," I begged in distressed.

This was the hardest thing I had ever done, and yet I realized with all that I am, that I needed to do this in my life. I was feeling wounded. As I struggled to walk, I could feel my body weighed down and not paying any attention to where I was going, I stumbled on a rock. Catching my fall, I went down on my knees and cried.

"Stay with me, Lord. You are my only hope. I need you," I shouted.

Gradually, my tears became less and less. I felt relief. I looked to see if there was anyone around. Being absolutely alone was depressing. The sun beat on me. I felt like wounded prey. The salt and sweat from my body poured out and filled every crack and crevice of me. The visor of my hat covered my face from the burning of the intense sun. I found my lip balm, uncapped it, and slowly applied it to my dried and cracked lips. It was smooth and soothing. I felt a little better now.

"I need to finish what I have started today," I said aloud to myself.

The stretch from Sansol to Viana seemed endless. I walked down a ravine, went through a tunnel, and followed pathways that eventually led me to cross over motorways. Today's walk was challenging. The real test was the blazing heat.

Seeing the town of Viana nearby, I leapt for joy. It inspired a fresh sense of hope. I stayed to rest. Washing my face with iced cold water made my body tingle and come alive all over. Goose bumps traveled my spine and back up my neck. I am alive. Water this cold in contrast to the heat made no sense to me right now.

Just before leaving Viana, I met a new person from Spain. I thought this was cool to walk the next nine kilometers with another new friend. She barely could speak English and nor I Spanish. Although we hardly understood each other, we both understood how awfully hot it was. We looked at each other and lifted our shoulders with a big sigh as if to say: "Oh well, let us do this."

When at long last we saw a sign announcing LOGROÑO on the side of a highway, we hugged each other in celebration. With great relief we cried out: "Bueno, Logroño!"

Not far down the road, I could see a woman stamping credentials. When we approached her, at first she did not seem too friendly. She looked as if she was tired and grumpy and had been stamping credentials all day in the draining heat. When it came my turn for a stamp, she walked away. I thought maybe she had decided to take a break. I waited patiently for a few minutes. When the woman came back, she brought with her a case of cold bottled water and handed it out to everyone. I took my bottle of water and pressed it around my face and neck. It felt so cool and refreshing. I smiled gratefully and thanked her. She stamped my credential and off I went into town.

When I entered Logroño, I spotted my friends right away. They were all sitting in the shade with their rucksacks next to them. One of my friends said aloud, "This albergue will only take us here in line. You will need to find another place."

"Okay, I will find another place," I replied. As I walked around the corner, I saw the friend with whom I walked earlier this morning.

"Is there a place for me here?" I asked.

"No, the numbers of pilgrims have filled this albergue for tonight," she replied.

I smiled and walked on. As I was walking, I saw more folks. If all the albergues are full tonight, where will those of us who do not have a place to stay sleep? I need to find a place and quickly.

A little way down the road, I saw a church. Perfect. I can rest there and then look for an albergue. I walked into Saint James Church. I sat down in the pew and rested for a bit. I began to pray for a place to stay tonight. Chances were slim since I walked into the town late. I could sense that I was not the only person in the church. I felt someone else there. I looked over my shoulder and saw a male coming up to me.

"If you need a place to stay tonight, Saint James Church has an albergue. There are not many beds in this albergue," the man said kindly.

I blinked my eyes twice to see if I was seeing and hearing things beyond the norm. When I opened my eyes, I thought I saw an angel.

"Yes, I do need a place to sleep tonight. Thank you," I replied.

He walked in front of me, took my hand, and led me to the front door of the albergue.

When we stepped inside, a gentleman took me to a small room. The room was empty. There were only four walls and a few windows. Before I could ask where the beds were, others were carrying cots into the room. It was awesome. After walking in from one of the hottest days so far, having this place to relax will be especially delightful.

I found showers and took a bath. As I was soaking, I felt my body gently absorbing the cool water. I had never before realized how amazing water could feel on my sunburned body. I felt clean and refreshed. Unfortunately, however, my knee began to ache again. I would need to ice it before I sleep. I washed out my clothes and hung them nearby my cot. The dry warm weather will dry them before I go to bed.

I heard noise down the hall. I followed the sounds and walked into a room full of friends. "Hola, Linda," they said in enthusiastic welcome.

BLISS

In a way, I felt as though I had come home. A woman took me by the hand and led me to the fiesta. I served myself and sat down to eat. I ate vegetables, fruits, drank a lot of water, and ate bread. After our meal, we shared our stories of the day, laughed, and sang songs.

Then I got up and went to the kitchen to see how I could help. Someone quickly handed me a dish towel and I got to work drying dishes. The men and women were just as exciting in the kitchen as outside in the eating area. We continued our laughter in the kitchen as we did our chores talking about our day, our events, and our challenges. Their facial reactions to the weather were funny.

Everyone agreed today was one of the hottest days. We were making fun of ourselves: the walking, the limping, and the staggering as we made our way to Logroño. Some of us were sunburned as well. We commiserated over our blisters and pains.

I remembered I needed to ice my knee tonight if I want to be able to walk at all tomorrow. When everything was done, I placed a few pieces of ice into a plastic bag and wrapped it in a towel, and made my way back to my cozy room. Climbing into my cot, I reflected back on today's journey. Placing the ice on my knee relieved the pain. I did my walk today. Folding my hands, I looked upward.

Stay with Me

"Thank you for staying with me. I am washed clean and I feel good again," I whispered. From an incredible sunrise to a near breakdown, and now a restful place to sleep tonight makes the journey worthwhile. Taking a deep breath and releasing it slowly, I realized tomorrow is around the corner.

As others walked into the room to find their cots, we wished each other a good night's sleep. Lights went out.

Day 9 ~ Nájera

Oasis

Today is Monday, July 30th. I got up early feeling very rested and ready to start my walk. After freshening up, I slipped out of the albergue and headed down the street. It was beginning to get light so I easily found my way out of Logroño. I saw the Camino marking and followed the path. After crossing through streets, a square, and an avenue, I came to an industrial area and a tunnel. Once through, the tunnel brought me out to an area of lush green trees. The smell of fresh greenery helped to give me energy to accomplish my goals for today.

"What is it that I hope for today?" I asked myself. "I want to walk twenty-six kilometers to Nájera."

As I thought this, I came upon a reservoir. Aha, I thought to myself, this is why the area smells so clean and fresh. I stopped for a little while and gazed upon the water. The shape of the reservoir was quite interesting. It looked like a closed fist of a left hand. The calmness brought peace to me. I closed my eyes and slowly breathed in the air. I held it inside me for as long as I could. Then I slowly released it. After doing this a couple of times, I decided it was time to move on.

Today is the third day of extreme heat. The rays of the sun are upon me like an overheated furnace. Sweat flowed down my body like a running river. I drank from my camelbak to replenish my output. Reaching into my jacket pocket, I pulled out a fig to eat. As I slowly ate the fig, its tiny tasty seeds were enough to fill me and satisfy my appetite. This will give me energy to climb through the bumpy terrain ahead.

As I began to climb uphill, I could feel my body being stretched all over. Walking is not a problem; however, my muscles ached from climbing. Cyclists are on the path today. Trying to dodge these cyclists may be my greatest challenge. Hearing bells would mean get out of the way or get run over. Although cyclists give walkers enough time to stop or walk to the side, it seemed like only mere seconds before cyclists passed by.

I heard a bell so I quickly moved to the shoulder part of the path. Before I could barely see the cyclist, it raced by and waved. The wave gave me a sense of satisfaction that I got out of the way at just the right time, even though it was close.

Coming to the town of Navarrete, I could see vineyards abundant with green grapes. This was a vineyard and perhaps there was a winery nearby. As I passed by the ruins of old buildings and arcades, the thought crossed my mind that perhaps this town was once an important place along the pilgrimage road. Long ago, hospices were built to help pilgrims on their passage. Today, I see ruins.

As I left Navarrete, I passed a cemetery. Again, a cyclist whizzed by. This time, the cyclist clipped my rucksack and caused me to spin in a circle. My walking stick left my hand and flew in the air. Instinctively, I closed my eyes. Dust whirled around me. I could taste it and feel it. When the dust settled, I carefully opened my eyes. I tried hard to see the cyclist. All I could see was a tiny figure in the far distance. The cyclist was gone forever. I would not see this person again. I thought today this path is not best for walkers, but for cyclists. I reached in my jacket for a cloth. I pulled it out, wet it, and wiped the dust from my face. I blew my nose. I felt awful. Nonetheless, I dusted myself off. I found my walking stick among the rubble and dirt. I picked it up. Putting one foot in front of the other, I prodded along. Be clam, I comforted myself, this will pass.

There were no longer trees in sight. The burning sun made the walking intolerable. A new suffering took hold during this part of the journey. It was almost mid-morning and it felt like late afternoon. The sun continued to beat down on my back. My hat covered my face, but it did not stop the heat. At last, I crossed a highway that took me into the village of Ventosa. I knew I could not stop here to rest if I wanted to be in Nájera near noon.

I saw someone on the side of the road. It was a friend, the physical therapist. He smiled at me.

"Hello, Linda. How are you? I have not seen you in a couple of days," he said.

"I am fine, just hot! Yes, we have not seen each other recently," I replied.

"How is your knee doing?" he asked.

"There was pain yesterday. So far, today there is no pain. When I finish my walk today, I will let you know. Are you going to Nájera?" I said.

"Yes, I am. If I see you there, I will look at your knee. See you then. Buen Camino," he replied.

I had some fresh hope after our encounter. I tread along. My knee will be looked at again and perhaps treated. If I am going to make it through the rest of this journey to Santiago de Compostela, the health of my knee is very important. It was so nice to see the young man again. I was reassured by my good fortune.

Climbing at this higher elevation required me to pick up my legs. The near miss was still fresh on my mind and I hoped not to encounter another cyclist for the rest of the day. The two earlier cyclists were more than enough to deal with for now.

Oasis

Once I reached Gravera, it would be downhill into Nájera. In the distance, I saw orchards. I walked under the shade of the trees for a while. It was delightful respite from the incessant sun. I walked across a highway that led me into Nájera.

Crossing over a long narrow bridge, I entered into the town of Nájera. I had successfully made my journey for today. I could see many folks all standing and sitting down upon the soft cool green grass. Trees were abundant alongside the river. As I turned the corner, I saw my friends relaxing near the water. To the right I spotted a little building. I thought to myself this could not be an albergue. But, yes, it was. My next thought was how will all these pilgrims fit into this little building? I am not going to worry about this right now. I placed my rucksack at the end of a long line near the albergue.

I walked over to see my friends. I felt a bit like a tortoise making its way to the end of the race. I was already anticipating that I would not have a place to stay tonight. I was anticipating that I would sleep outside under the moon and stars. I am prepared. One of my friends called me over to sit with them. There were others I knew enjoying the shade under a beautiful big tree. I wriggled my tired body in between two friends. We felt glued to the tree. It felt so good to sit down and relax, while waiting until the albergue opened later in the afternoon. We had another two hours to R&R.

I looked for the young gentleman who was going to look at my knee. I did not spot him amidst the crowd. I thought maybe he went on to another village, knowing how small this one is. If I do not run into him here, then at the very least, I will again need to ice my knee this evening before I go to bed.

Needing to hydrate, I reached for my camelbak. Water tastes so good when I am this thirsty. Breathing deeply, I closed my eyes. I heard the beautiful sound of running water from a nearby stream. The cool breezes lightened my mood and helped to ease my tired body. I dozed for a little while. Everyone was very quiet. We all wanted to unwind from our tiring hikes. The flow of the river continued to soothe and comfort us.

After a while, I opened my eyes, seeing the river before me. If there is no room in the albergue, I will sleep outside near this river. Having the river next to me would be great therapy. I could embrace nature tonight under the moon and stars.

"The albergue is open," someone announced. "Get in line to check-in." Everyone seemed to get up gingerly. It took me a while before I made my way into the line.

"There are not many beds in this place," the albergue caretaker said.

"What good will it does for me to stay in this line? After all, I am nearly the last one in line," I mumbled. Then I felt a little internal nudge.

"Stay in line," my inner voice whispered.

At this point, I figured there was nothing to lose, so I made up my mind to stay to see what will happen. The worst case scenario would be that I would sleep outside. Sleeping under the moon and stars next to a river may not be so bad after all. At least, it will be nice and cool.

As I made my way through the front door and to the counter, I noticed some folks were not being checked in. I tried to see what was happening. Then one of the hospitality personnel looked at me and began to speak in English.

"Are you a cyclist? Are you traveling with a light gear? Have you given your full gear to a van driver or someone to be brought here?" she asked.

"No, I am a walker. I am walking with my full rucksack. I have not given my gear to anyone. Why do you ask?" I replied.

"All cyclists and those with light gear are asked to wait until all full gear walkers are checked in. Then we will open it up to everyone else," she responded.

Without hesitating, the nice woman took my credential and stamped it. I paid a few euros and walked through a doorway. I found my bunk for the night. I quickly made my way to the showers to wash my stinky body.

After washing up, I went back to sit by the river for a while longer. The cool evening air and sweet sounds of flowing water inspired me sit and just stare for a while.

It was an oasis. The tranquility relaxed me deeply. The hike today was fine, but the heat was sweltering.

"This is great! I have a place to stay tonight. Patience is indeed a virtue," I thought. Then I heard footsteps. I turned around and saw six friends walking toward me.

"Linda, it is dinner time. We are going to find a place. Please join us," a friend said.

"Sure, I would love to. I am hungry. Thank you for the invitation," I replied.

Getting up, I joined the group. Not too far from the albergue, we found a little place to eat. We drank lots of water. The food was simple and delicious and the company was delightful. Some of my friends had the regional wine as well. We shared our experiences of the day, particularly those encounters with the cyclists that zoomed by nearly missing many of us. We spent the evening filled with simple laughter, all pleased that we had come through another day.

After a delightful dinner, we made our way back to the albergue. The night seemed perfect. Meandering alongside the river and looking up into the heavens lent us to a silent walk back.

Although today's trekking may have been a bit perilous, it was also awesome. Ending up together in this lovely village of Nájera made any challenges we faced throughout the day disappear. Tonight Nájera is a perfect oasis in the midst of this journey.

Day 10 ~ Santo Domingo de la Calzada

Morning Dew

Departing Nájera early in the morning saddened me a little. I am leaving behind a precious oasis in the middle of my journey. Nájera holds a special place in my heart. It is a place of peace and comfort for me. After a long hard week of trekking, I found a sweet little paradise in this town.

Many hikers got up at the same time today. Cirueña will be the highest summit to climb so far. Then there will be about six kilometers before reaching Santo Domingo de la Calzada. This place is named after a hermit by the name Santo Domingo. He lived in the eleventh century. He was crafty in architectural design as well as a skilled builder. He built a bridge over the Oja River for pilgrims to cross, leading to a church and a resting place.

Seeing a spectacular sunrise this morning fills me with extra energy. As the sun rises from behind a range of mountains, the glow stretches across the entire area causing everything to appear golden and still. This beauty starts the day perfectly for me. I am able to see Mother Earth awaken from her slumber. The morning air is fresh and cool.

As I begin hiking to the first peak of this mountain, I can see in the distance the village of Azofra. From atop the mountain, I see the morning dew resting on this little town. I walk down into a valley and up again before reaching the village. I wondered if I would make it in time to experience the coolness of the morning there. I will need to travel five kilometers before arriving. If I am going to get there before the heat sets in, then I need to pick up my pace and walk faster. I do not want to miss the treat of morning freshness in this small town.

Climbing up the next peak is not too difficult. The elevation is less steep and the surface levels off. Before I knew it, I reached my destination. The wetness and moist air gives me goose bumps and tingles throughout my body. I am so comfortable that I could stay here the rest of the day. Taking off my hat, I could feel the wetness in my hair. It is delightful. I closed my eyes and I breathed in deeply cooling my already tired body.

After a while, I slowly strolled through the small town. As I ate a piece of bread, I saw a water fountain nearby. I went to drink from it. The water is cold and refreshing. This awoke me from my ecstasy. I knew I needed to start walking again if I am going to make it to Santo Domingo de la Calzada by midday.

Leaving the village of Azofra, I could sense something is different. My inner burden somehow seems lighter. There seems to be no weight on my shoulders from my rucksack anymore. There is no pain in my knee. It is a brief moment of personal relief.

As I walked along, it very quickly began to sizzle in the heat of the direct sun. I need to find shade quickly. So much for feeling light today. For the fourth straight day, it has been sweltering.

A bit farther up the path, I see a large herd of sheep grazing in an open field. There is no fencing to keep them in. Interesting, no fence, and yet the sheep stays together without any rumblings. No escaping from the pack. I waited for the next passer-by to see if they could take a picture of me by the sheep. As I waited, I stared at the sheep. They look so meek and humble. I can see a wheat field on another hillside. It laid a golden thin blanket of color onto the scene. I heard footsteps. I glanced over. A person is walking toward me. I waved for her to stop.

"Do you speak English?" I asked.

"A little bit," she replied.

"Could you please take a picture of me with the sheep?" I asked again.

"Sure, of course!" she answered.

Standing with my stick stretched away from my left side, I posed and smiled. After taking my picture, the woman and I talked and walked together for a little while. The companionship helped our walk go more quickly to the next town. Meeting new people along the way always makes the day seem less tiring.

We heard the sound of small bells in the distance. As we turned to look back, we could see cyclists coming toward us. I instinctively jumped over to her side of the roadway to make way for the speeding cyclists. We attached ourselves to one another. We pointed our heads toward the ground and we kept our eyes closed until the sounds of the tires disappeared.

"Hola! Buen Camino," the cyclists shouted as they zoomed by.

That was too close for our safety. We counted about eleven in the cluster. What a whirlwind day for cyclists. As the day went on there were more and more cyclists. I lost count after six groups passed us by.

"What is next? A sheep stampede," the woman joked.

"Oh, please do not even think that. We could be trampled by the size of the sheep herd," I responded.

We dusted ourselves off and we wiped our faces with washcloths we had moistened. Focusing on the trail became a discipline of survival. We kept our silence until we reached Cirueña.

When at last we approached Cirueña, we noticed a hospital for traveling pilgrims had been built there. Today, not much of it stands. The town is quiet and charming.

"My feet are sore. I have blisters so I need to rest," my friend confessed.

"I am sorry to hear this. Do you want me to stay with you until you feel better?" I asked her.

"No. You go ahead on your own. I will meet you in Santo Domingo de la Calzada," she quietly responded.

We sat for a little while and had lunch. Afterward, I picked up my rucksack and my stick. I looked at my friend.

"Are you sure you are going to be all right alone? I could stay with you?" I offered.

"No, no. You move along and I will catch up. Buen Camino," she said.

"Take care. Buen Camino," I replied. I walked away slowly and waved good-bye.

"I will see you later. Okay?" she reassured me.

I smiled at her and walked on. I hope she will be fine.

As I left Cirueña, I kept thinking about my friend. At least, we are only about six kilometers to Santo Domingo de la Calzada. The walking path has turned to gravel. This makes it even more of a challenge to walk. The dry grass on the hillside looks brittle and hot.

Up the trail, I saw about twenty hikers ahead of me. Some are walking together and others alone. These last kilometers are up and down foothills. It is oppressively hot. As I arrived at the top of a hill, bells went off. I looked back. This time a very large group of cyclists came zooming by. The rocks from the roadway went flying. I buried my head and covered my face.

I made a decision in the moment to keep going and not feel sorry for myself. I demanded myself to keep alert and accept the situation. I kept walking. I needed to share this path with the cyclists. I stayed humble and picked up my feet as I paced my steps.

Upon entering Santo Domingo de la Calzada, I found the local cathedral. A priest shared about a story that happened here.

The story goes that there was a German couple and their young son walking the pilgrimage road to Santiago de Compostela. They had spent the night at Santo Domingo de la Calzada. An innkeeper's daughter had fallen in love with the couple's son. She made proposals to the young man. He did not befriend her. Since he rejected her, she hid a silver cup in the young man's sack. She contacted the authorities and the young man was arrested, jailed, and then hung for the crime. Leaving the corpse of the young man to rot demonstrated to all who passed the steep price of stealing. The loss of the couple's son brought great distress to his parents. Nevertheless, they continued their pilgrimage to Santiago de Compostela.

On the way back from their journey, the parents stopped at Santo Domingo de la Calzada. They visited the gallows where their deceased son was hanged. To their surprise and delight, the son that they thought had been hanged greeted them! He told his parents Santo Domingo held his feet while he was hanging. The couple went to find the chief authority that was having a roasted rooster and hen for dinner. At hearing the news that the young man was alive, the hen and the rooster began to cluck and crow.

Today, a rooster and a hen are in a henhouse inside the cathedral. Throughout the day, the rooster will crow and the hen clucks. They are located way at the back of the cathedral high above the floor. This is the first time I had seen animals inside a cathedral. Pretty cool! This is a highlight for the day.

As I made my way out the cathedral, I began walking down a narrow road.

"Am I seeing things? Is this who I think it is? She made it!" I declared with delight.

"Hello, hello," I said cheerfully. The woman turned and smiled. "I am so glad you made it. Are you all right?" I asked.

"I am sore and tired," she replied.

"Well, I have not found an albergue as yet. Do you want to see if we could find one?" I asked.

"Yes, that would be fine," she smiled.

The albergue is not far away. Teaming up with a new friend is wonderful. At the albergue, a sister stamped our credentials. We found our beds, showered, and washed our filthy clothes. I iced my knee and rested for a few hours.

Later during the evening, I walked around the town. I met some old friends I had not seen in a week. It is wonderful. We made our way to a little market and picked up bread and fruits. Buying vegetables for dinner was special. When we returned to the albergue, we found the kitchen. We cut up the veggies, sat around a large table, and shared a meal. While we were eating, we heard music and the sound of a flute. Sure enough, another friend who plays the flute joined our company. We laughed and shared our adventures about the many cyclists we encountered for the day. At least for this night, no bike bells rang, no dust whirled around, and no rocks flew in the air.

After dinner, we made our way to the cathedral and attended evening Mass. Reflecting on the experiences of the day I realized how lucky I am to do what I am doing. I am humbled and in awe by all that has happened. Yes, I may have some fixing up to do inside of me, but I am all right. I am trying to be a better person.

This is the beauty of going to Mass. I ask forgiveness, and I come to give thanks and praise for all what I have and do not have. As a pilgrim, I strive to do the best I can from day-to-day. Why? Because NOW is all I have. Anything more for now would be too much.

As we left the cathedral, we quietly walked back to the albergue. The evening feels nice. As I look up at the stars and sky, I have hope for tomorrow. I may not have walked as quickly as I would have liked, but in the end, I made it and I am not alone. Friends give each other hope. Without hope, what is there to strive for in my life? Hope is with me yesterday, today, and tomorrow.

Milestone

Although I am starting out a little later this morning, I feel energetic. Getting out of my bunk and making my way to the bathroom is becoming a ritual. After freshening up, I waited patiently for the large ancient iron double doors to open. As I stood waiting, some of my friends joined me. For most of us, our destination for today is Belorado. This is about twenty-two kilometers from here. I am not going to worry about the weather today. One more day of heat hardly matters anymore.

An elderly sister of the cloth walked passed us wearing her black habit. She was heading toward the great iron doors. As she reached into her pocket, she took out a large iron skeleton key to unlock the doors. The clunking sound as the key turned signaled that soon we will be on our way. Walking outside I could feel the sunlight warm my body. I am ready to begin.

Passing the cathedral, I heard the rooster crow and the hen clucking. The story of this little town is fascinating. I am eager to hear these stories and legends of ancient times.

As I was leaving Santo Domingo de la Calzada, I walked over a stone bridge built by Santo Domingo. This bridge crossed over the Oja River. An engineer, Santo Domingo had built roads and bridges for trekkers. Approaching the stone bridge, I walked gingerly, thinking how amazing this bridge is still standing after all these years. After making my way to the other side, I looked back to see the beauty of the old walls and the narrow roads of the quaint town.

After walking an hour in the sunlight, I approached a meadow of sunflowers. I walked into the heart of the meadow. The centers of the sunflowers are as big as my face. The green stems and healthy leaves stood tall and strong. Behind the sunflowers was a manicured hill of golden wheat. I touched the rich yellow petals of one of the flowers. The smell aroused my senses. I closed my eyes and delighted at the sweet aroma. I imagined that I was a sunflower with big yellow petals, a bright shiny face, sturdy and strong, enough to withstand the heat of the blazing sun. Standing among the sunflowers brought me joy and gladness. This experience inspired me to vow to be cheerful to others and to myself. Pleased, I stepped out of the meadow and started to walk.

After passing through woodland, I came to the rural village of Grañón. Like Santo Domingo de la Calzada, this village has ancient structures and narrow ways. I stopped to rest and drink water. I felt bright and eager, like one of the sunflowers that inspired me earlier this morning. Even though the heat of the sun was intense, I felt strong to walk my journey filled with vim and vigor.

I made my way to Redecilla del Camino and Castildelgado. The hike gradually started becoming more challenging as I began ascending to higher ground. Cyclists were around as well. They did not bother me today. Whereas yesterday I was nearly hit, today I welcomed the cyclists. I found it easy to remember the sunflowers and stay bright and positive for now.

In a distance, I could see the village of Viloria de Rioja. This is the birthplace of Santo Domingo. Walking into a valley, I came upon the little town. I went inside the parish church. There can be found a baptismal fountain where the saint was baptized. After praying for a little while, I stepped outside and ate my lunch. This is a significant day, finding the birthplace of this saint. I am realizing on the Camino I am not only seeking myself, but others such as Santo Domingo.

BLISS

Leaving Viloria de Rioja, I came across a tall red and white sign. The top of the sign read Junta de Castilla y León El Camino de Santiago en Castilla y León. I felt good. I am pointed toward Belorado, just where I need to go today. Although Belorado was at the bottom of the sign, this is a high point for me today. I will have many more kilometers to hike. There is no turning back now.

As I continued walking, I saw some folks I had not seen in a while. We stopped, talked, and carried out our walk together. Quite suddenly, the weather became cooler.

"Is it cool or is this my imagination?" I asked.

"Yes, it is cooler. It is not your imagination," someone replied. "We are near a stream. The weather is cooler here. The trees are giving us shade and comfort."

"I hope it is like this the rest of the way to Belorado," I responded.

"It will be because we are almost there," she answered.

We found ourselves smiling the rest of our way into Belorado. Looking around we could see ruins. Years ago, many hostels were in this little town to accommodate pilgrims on their journey.

Finding the albergue is not a problem because it is in front of us. I placed my rucksack in line. As I sat, I felt a slight breeze. This cooled me off. Then I could hear birds chirping. Taking a deep breath, I drank in this beautiful day.

"Did you come from Santo Domingo de la Calzada? Did you spend the night there?" a volunteer asked. There were about twenty-five of us checking in.

"Yes," we all said.

"Do you have bed bugs?" another volunteer asked.

"No. We do not have bed bugs," we replied.

"We heard Santo Domingo de la Calzada has bed bugs. We will check everyone before checking in. If we find bed bugs, you will need to go to the next village. Do not bring bed bugs to Belorado. We run a clean albergue here," a volunteer insisted.

I thought this is not what we need now—bed bugs. I do not have bed bugs, but what if my rucksack does. When my turn came, they checked my head, body, clothing, walking stick, shoes, hat, and rucksack.

"Come. You can stay here tonight," a volunteer said roughly.

"Yeah, no bed bugs," I said. Then I quickly give him my credential before he changed his mind. He stamped it.

Around the corner, I saw Saint Marie Church. Before I go to church, I need to do my routine. Taking a nap in the afternoons has become essential for me. I find when I do, I feel more refreshed in the evenings. So I plopped myself on my bunk. Without any hesitation, I promptly fell asleep. After napping, I walked to a little market to pick up some bread and fruit for my journey tomorrow. I made my way back to the albergue to drop off my food.

Finding a church is always a pleasure. As I walked into the church, I saw a few familiar faces. No sooner than I sat down, Mass began. I was filled with joy to attend Mass after a long day's walk. Reflecting back on today's journey, I recalled the sunflowers in the meadow and how being there was a turning point for me on this walk. As we listened to the homily by the priest, I could not understand what he said. The Mass was in Spanish. That was fine with me. During the Mass, the priest said a prayer and blessed all pilgrims. This is special. The Holy Spirit will give us the strength to continue this journey.

After Mass, I asked a friend, "What was the message in today's homily?"

"The homily was about Jesus being the light of the world. If we walk with Jesus we do not walk in darkness, but in the light," my friend replied.

"I started my day as a sunflower walking in the light. Toward the end, I reached a milestone," I humbly thought. This is good news. It never ceases to amaze me how the day starts and how it ends. The connection is simply incredible. Walking in the light of Jesus instead of darkness may be simple, but it can be difficult at times. I am a child of light, if I choose to walk in it.

It was humbling walking back to the albergue after Mass. During dinner, we shared a meal. We ate pasta, tossed salad, and fruit, complimented with the regional wine as well. After dinner, everyone kept quiet for a long while.

"Linda, why are you doing the Camino?" a friend asked.

"I am doing the Camino to find myself so that I could be a better person. Every day I am learning a little bit more about me. I am asking for forgiveness for the wrongs I have done in my life. Walking the Camino, I am beginning to have a deeper relationship with Jesus. I am also making new friends along the way. Seeing the different villages is always exciting. Each village is one of a kind," I replied. I asked my friend the same question.

"I do not know yet. I am still seeking and searching as to why I am doing the Camino. Maybe one day I will know. I hope to find an answer soon," my friend responded.

Making my way back to my bunk, I looked in my rucksack. It is time to reorganize my things. Separating everything, I decided I wanted to give two T-shirts and dental floss to the volunteers. This would help the next pilgrim on their journey if they needed something to wear and a personal hygiene and this will also lighten my rucksack. After today, it is time to keep things more simple and down-to-earth. I gave a volunteer my little supplies.

"Here is something for another person who is walking this way. Could you please give it to someone who needs fresh supplies?" I asked.

At first, the volunteer looked at me quizzically. "Well, okay. This is most thoughtful of you. Buen Camino," he replied.

"By the way, do you have any ice? I need it for my knees," I inquired.

"We do not have ice. How about two frozen bags of peas?" he offered.

"I think those will work," I accepted. When I got to my bunk, I applied the frozen bags on my knees. After a while, I returned them to the volunteer.

"Thank you," I said.

"You are welcome. Are your knees better?" he asked.

"Yes, they will be ready to do the walk tomorrow. Good night," I answered.

As I snuggled in my bunk, I kept thinking about the sunflowers and milestone I encountered today. The beauty and strength in the sunflowers inspired me to walk. The fields soften the way. Then I thought a sunflower's radiating beauty is here for a little while. Over time, it will die and fade way. Gentle coolness from the rivers today reduced the sun's heat. These milestones give me hope to continue hiking.

Milestone

Today I learned something. I need to stop, look, and listen. I think I see things in a different light now. I can take off my blinders and see more of what is around me. I have come to accept my mistakes in life. These mistakes are through my human weakness. I am not perfect. I am not strong, but with my God, all things are possible.

As I walk this road, I do not fear. My strength carries me through fields, foothills, valleys, mountaintops, and across bridges every day. This strength is not from me, but from my God. Passing through villages day after day, I am not burdened. The sun's blazing heat no longer makes me weary.

Hikers are here in this albergue for an overnight stay. We are tired from today, but tomorrow will be here before we know it. Our exhausted bodies, minds, and spirits will rest for now. The food we eat will sustain us as we walk tomorrow. In the morning, we will get up and be on our way to the next place. As we leave tomorrow, we go our separate ways and in a couple of days, we may see each other again. The goal is to reach the end. If some of us do not make it, we can come back and pick up from where we left off.

Day 12 ~ San Juan de Ortega

Garlic Soup

Stepping outside the albergue this morning, I noticed that the weather seemed cooler than yesterday. I was a little afraid to walk today. Although I am prepared for crossing over the Oca hills, the path can be arduous. The elevation is 1,150 meters. I will need to be extremely focused today because hikers have lost their way through these hills, and the area has wild animals. Even if I wanted to, I cannot stay in Belorado. The next group of pilgrims will be coming here today so I need to move on.

After walking a while, I entered into a village. I suddenly felt a Mother Nature attack. I needed to find a restroom fast. Passing by little stores, I saw an eatery. I ran into the place and saw a restroom sign. I knocked on the door and a woman responded. If I do not go now, something drastic will happen, like doing it in my pants. I turned and saw the men's restroom. I knocked on the door. There was no answer. I opened the door and rushed through another doorway then locked it behind me. Shortly after relieving myself, I heard a noise.

"Yikes, I think perhaps I am not here alone," I whispered. I opened the door slowly and peered out. Suddenly I looked in the mirror and I saw a man. "Sorry," I politely said.

He looked at me and jumped slightly at the unexpected sight of a woman in the men's restroom. Without hesitating, I smiled and walked out. Seeing the look or amazement on his face confirmed my being there was more shocking for him than it was for me. That was close, but I was not bothered because I needed to use the facilities. At times, Mother Nature puts me in strange places.

Stepping outside of the eatery, I took a deep breath expelling a sigh of relief and began to walk. Now, I am ready to finish this journey today.

Leaving Tosantos, I continued on my way to Villambistia. Many trees provided shade and comfort. The soreness in my knee started again. It throbbed painfully. I looked around to see where I could stop and rest my leg. Seeing a large stone, I walked over to sit on it. As I was sitting on the rock, I heard noises in the wooden area nearby.

"Get ready for this. What is it? What could it be?" I coached myself. "I am not going to move. Today, I am a stone. Be still, keep quiet, and do not move," I willed. My back was facing the trees. I could not see what was coming. I turned slowly. It was a hiker coming out of the woods. He showed a peace sign.

"Peace to you," I said. "Why are you coming out of the woods?" I asked.

"I took the wrong turn and I got lost," he answered.

"I love your peace sign. When I heard the noises, I did not know what to think. I am so glad it is you and nothing else because I would not know how to handle it. At the time, I pretended to be this rock," I said with a sigh of relief.

We walked together until we reached Espinosa del Camino. When we arrived in the village, we said Buen Camino to each other. He stayed in the village while I decided to walk on. Through the excitement, I made a new friend today. On this journey, we need to be ready for the unexpected. Little did the man know he would run into me and vice-versa. The rest of way I walked with opened eyes. This is an adventure.

The pathway connected alongside a roadway. Crossing over and back took me through villages until I reached my last crossing, Villafranca-Montes de Oca. The climb took me into the hills. I could feel the hike becoming strenuous. Today, I will need courage and strength. My feet and knee ached. I could feel the back of my legs stretching as I lugged myself up the hills. Taking one step at a time, I called out to God.

"Help me to do this. You are my strength. I cannot do it alone," I said. As I continued walking, I could feel my feet being lifted. "Yes, Lord. You are kind and merciful. All things are possible. With you, there is no hurt and fear," I said fervently.

Walking into San Juan de Ortega, I saw a few friends sitting on benches in the shade. They were enjoying their lunch.

"You made it, Linda," a friend shouted.

Limping like a wounded puppy, all I could do was smile for the moment. "Yes, it is good to be here," I said. Looking over to the side, I saw a couple that I had met on the first day of the walk.

"Good to see you again, Linda," the man said.

"Yes, it is good to see you, too. How are you?" I answered.

"We are doing fine. Although we are tired, we are glad to be here. This is a pretty place," he replied.

"Are you staying here tonight?" I asked.

"No, we are going to another village after lunch," he responded. "Do you want to join us?"

"Thank you, but I am going to stay here. I have heard about the delicious garlic soup so I want to try it tonight," I answered.

I looked at the façade of San Juan de Ortega Church. This is so beautiful. Three bells were above the church and a cross rested on top of the façade. The church is built of stone probably many years ago. Turning my head, I saw an open doorway. I walked over to it and saw an elderly man sitting in a chair. Entering through the doorway, I saw another chair. It was empty, so I sat down. The man leaned over the little table and looked at me.

"Are you staying here tonight?" he asked.

"I would like to. Is this an albergue?" I inquired.

"Yes, it is an old monastery," he said.

"I will stay here," I replied feeling drained. I gave him my credential, which he stamped and I paid him the required euro. I have a place to stay tonight.

The man stood up and walked me through another doorway into a large room filled with bunk beds. I walked over to the window and put my rucksack on a bunk. I am here for tonight.

Walking outside, I saw a little tavern. I think I will go and see what they have. When I entered the bar, I noticed it was empty. A small man and woman were behind the counter. "I would like to eat and drink something here," I said. I saw a table next to a window. I pointed to it indicating that I would like to sit there. The man nodded his head in approval. I walked over to the table and gently sat down on a wooden chair. There is no sitting down quickly these days since my body feels as stiff and hard as a rock. Taking it easy and slow is the way to go now, especially after walking seven hours today.

The woman gave me a menu. I ordered a sandwich, orange juice, and water. This will be my lunch for today. After eating, I made my way back to the albergue. I heard laughter as I walked into the room. I saw many teenagers. They were from France. Some were sleeping and others were talking. Rucksacks were at the heads and feet of bunk beds. Towels hung over the bunk frames and assorted chairs were layered with blankets.

"I guess it is going to be cold tonight," I thought. The walls and columns needed painting, but it is cozy. After the monastery closed, it turned into a place for pilgrims to come, sleep, and rest.

After showering, I walked over to the church. San Juan de Ortega is buried here. It is said that he and Santo Domingo built this church. San Juan lived mostly in the Oca hills and built bridges and hospices.

This church is famous because of one of the architectural features. It shows the Annunciation of Mary and the Visitation of Mary and Elizabeth. The carved stone artwork is on columns standing next to one another. Looking up at the scene, I could see smiles on the faces of the people in the architectural design. The Annunciation is the scene where the angel appears to Mary. The angel says to Mary that she will be the mother of Jesus. The Visitation scene is where Mary visits Elizabeth. Both women are with child. Mary stays with Elizabeth for three months. During the equinox on March 20th and September 20th, evening sunlight shines on these two scenes.

This artwork was discovered in 1974. The sun continues to shines on these two events. An inspiration came into my mind. "Wow, this would be stunning to see on March 20th. It is my birthday," I said cheerfully. Then I walked back to the albergue to take a nap.

After a splendid rest, I awoke to the sounds of some of the young teenagers up from their nap as well. Looking at my watch, I realized it was time to go to Mass. Making my way over to the church, I could see people walking passed San Juan de Ortega. I wanted to stop and say to them, "Do not walk any further. Spend the night here. Inside the church there is something beautiful to see." Then I thought perhaps they might want to continue walking.

"Go inside the church," a little voice whispered to me.

"Yes, I am going," I replied.

When I entered the church, I was surprised to see the elderly man who checked me into the albergue vested as a priest.

"Oh, gosh!" I thought. I did not realize at the time that I was being checked in here that he is a priest. It is good. I am at Mass. At the end of Mass, the priest blessed all the pilgrims.

After Mass, everyone walked over to the hall to have garlic soup. Other pilgrims who have stayed overnight here have raved about this soup. We were all seated when blue and white cups were brought in and placed at the end of the table. A woman carrying the garlic soup placed a large red pot next to the soup cups. Then the priest walked through the narrow doorway. The priest blessed the soup. He picked up a metal ladle and began to serve us.

When I got my garlic soup, I took a sniff. The aroma rose into my nostrils, stimulating my appetite. I began to salivate. I could almost taste the soup already. I slowly spooned the soup to my mouth.

"Wow, this is delicious," I said.

A person sitting next to me said, "Yes, it is delicious!" We all looked at each other and rolled our eyes in delight. Everyone smiled.

After the priest served everyone, he sat down with us. "I am glad you like the garlic soup," he said.

"Thank you. This is delicious," we said in delight.

"We have been serving this soup for many years. San Juan de Ortega is known for its delicious garlic soup," he replied.

This morning I was a little afraid, but I trusted. Meeting someone coming from the woods helped me to awaken to see with a broader perspective. The rugged terrain across the Oca hills was tiring, but I made it. Then to be here in San Juan de Ortega made my day worthwhile. I have come to know this much; that the challenges I face in life are for my growth.

There are some places special enough that I want to return to them and San Juan de Ortega is such a place. My goal is to return on March 20th.

Day 13 ~ Burgos

Gratitude

At half-past five in the morning, I began to walk. Outside of the albergue it is dark. The weather feels fresh. The morning crispness has awakened me from my sleep. The cool air smacks me on my face and wakes me up to a new day. I like walking in the dark because it brings me peace. This is the quietest time of the day for me.

Suddenly, I heard a voice.

"Wrong direction," someone said.

I thought I was hearing things so I kept walking.

"Wrong direction," the voice said again.

By this time, I thought I am not hearing things, but I am sure this is the right way.

Finally, the voice shouted, "You are going in the wrong direction."

I turned around and walked back. A flicker of light shone in a distance. It is a flashlight. As I was getting closer to the light, I could see a man and woman standing before me.

"Where are you headed?" the man inquired.

"I am on my way to Burgos. Am I going in the wrong direction?" I asked.

"Yes. Go this way. We are also on our way to Burgos. Please look at the sign. The arrow is pointing in the opposite direction from where you were headed," he said kindly.

"My goodness, I must still be asleep. Thank you," I replied.

"Buen Camino," the couple said.

"Once again, thank you for setting me straight this morning. Buen Camino to you as well," I said with gratitude.

Golly, that could have been a disaster, I thought. I have heard folks hiking and mistakenly walking in the direction and getting extremely lost. Be watchful. Keep your eyes on the direction of the marking, I reminded myself.

The couple walked ahead of me. I tried to keep up with them, but they were faster than I. As it was still dark, their light kept me on the path behind them. Soon dawn was upon us. To the east I could see the sunlight breaking over the mountain range. In the distance, I saw a little village that sat upon a hill. As I am approaching the village, the weather is nice, but this is still early in the morning and anything could happen. The spectacular sunrise brought light. Everywhere around it is awakening to a beautiful day. As I passed by, I heard roosters crowing and dogs barking.

After leaving the village, in the near distance I spotted a cross. This is interesting. I stopped for little while. Then I saw a marker leading into a wooded area. Entering into the area, I could feel the coolness. I wished the rest of the day could be like this. My mind is clear of all things. Walking seemed so easy. The plants are lush and green, and the scent of pine is all around. Goodness and kindness are all around.

"Thank you, Lord. You know my heart," I said softly.

Then I recalled Psalm 139:1-6. This is one of my favorite Psalms.

O Lord, you have searched me and known me,
You know when I sit down and when I rise up;
  you discern my thoughts from far away.
You search out my path and my lying down,
  and are acquainted with all my ways.
Ever before a word is on my tongue,
  O Lord, you know it completely.
You hem me in, behind and before,
  and lay your hand upon me.
Such knowledge is too wonderful for me;
  it is so high that I cannot attain it.

Silence is all around now. If only this could be forever, I would not need to be concerned about anything. Stepping with one leg in front of the other made me feel as I was walking on a cloud. Taking gentle steps through the wooded area gave me a feeling it is eternal. I am in awe. Then I kicked a rock. My feeling of the everlasting ended abruptly. I fell to the ground on all fours.

I picked up myself from the ground. I brushed all the leaves and scrubs from my jacket and pants. "Now, why did I have to go and do that Miss Messy?" I asked myself. "If you want to reach Burgos today, you need to continue your journey," I chuckled.

Hearing footsteps come from behind, I stepped aside as someone passed by.

"Buen Camino," I said. The man looked back and smiled.

"Buen Camino to you," he said and waved.

As I looked up, he was climbing a hill. On the hill was another cross. "This is interesting. Two crosses today," I said excitingly.

Looking over to the side, I saw a little village ahead. There is Agés. Walking into the town, I looked around. This town is small and quaint. There is not much to see here except an old hermitage. I did not want to stop here. I continued on strolling through the town. It will be another two kilometers before reaching Atapuerca.

Gratitude

Crossing over a bridge built by San Juan reminded me of the delicious garlic soup I had last night.

As I left Atapuerca, I found a third cross. This time it was large and wooden. As I reached it, I stopped to notice a pile of rocks around the cross. I surmised that as folks passed by, they would put rocks around the cross. My thoughts were correct. A couple came up behind me put two stones on the pile. They smiled at me and continued on. I looked around and found a little smooth pebble. I picked it up and put it on the pile nearest to the cross.

"I feel blessed. I came upon three crosses today," I whispered solemnly. Since I have been on the journey, I have not seen three crosses in one day. Maybe God is telling me something. I feel the need to be still and quiet.

Feeling hungry, I reached into my jacket and pulled out a plum and started to eat it. As I bit into the plum, it squirted my face. It tasted ripe and juicy. Being purple today would not matter. I reached into my pocket again and pulled out a few dates. They were tasty, but sticky. "Aha, being purple and sticky makes a good combination," I chuckled to myself. No one would see me, and if they did, they would not recognize me.

As I reached the peak of Matagrande, I rested for a little bit. Descending will be nice, especially today.

Burgos is at a lower altitude and the walk will take less endurance. Although my feet and knee did not hurt as much today, when I reach Burgos, I decided to buy some anti-inflammatory ointment. Burgos will be one of the last stops in which I could pick up some type of ointment. I will also see if they have a knee brace just in case I will need one later, I will have it on hand. Not many villages have a pharmacy, but Burgos is a big city. They will have a pharmacy.

Crossing over a highway, led me back on the path. Many years ago, these highways were not around. It did not make it difficult to walk to get over to the other side. There was no other side. Once highways were built, hikers need to be careful in crossing the roads. Drivers are cautious when they see a pilgrim walking across the highways. They will slow down and stop to let them cross. This is very respectful.

The city of Burgos is not to be missed. It is large. A famous cathedral is in Burgos. I reached the entry and as I walked into the city, I saw two young women staring at me.

"Are you walking the Camino?" one of them asked me.

"Yes, I am. How about you?" I asked.

"We are walking it as well," they replied.

"Good. Let us walk into the town together. We can be a threesome," I said.

"Yes, this will be good," they responded.

As we walked into the city, we saw many shops. Those living in the city looked at us as if we were strange. "Pilgrims are here," some would say.

Then one of the women said she needed to stop by the next pharmacy to pick up some medication.

"May I go with you?" I asked.

"Sure, what is it you need?" she replied.

"I need some anti-inflammatory ointment and a knee brace," I answered.

A pharmacy was not too far away. We went inside and picked up what we needed. I felt better having ointment and a knee brace just in case I need it later. Then we walked through the entire city until we reached the albergue.

"This is a large albergue. It is cabana style," I said.

"Yes, this is quite big," the women replied.

I thanked the women for walking with me and taking me to the pharmacy. We said our good-byes and wished each other a Buen Camino.

After being stamped in and paying for my stay, a young man took me to my cabin. He showed me where the restrooms were and where I could wash my clothes. I felt delighted with the treatment I received by this albergue. I quickly showered and washed my clothes. Hanging my clothes became an adventure. The lines were all used.

"How am I going to hang my clothes? There is no room on these lines. Where are my safety pins?" I asked myself. I found my pins and began hanging my clothes. Fastening the pins to my clothing then clipping them to the line was a perfect solution. It is a windy day and in no time, my clothes will be dry.

I decided to nap for part of the afternoon. Applying the ointment to my knee relieved the soreness. The noise inside the albergue did not bother me. Tucking my rucksack under my feet, I fell soundly asleep.

After a good deep rest, I got up and went outside to gather my clothes. As predicted, they were dry. I freshened up, walked out of the albergue and headed toward the cathedral. As I walked inside the cathedral, I met a friend I had not seen in two days. It was so nice to see her again.

"It is good to see you. How is your leg doing?" I asked.

"My leg still hurts, but not as much," she responded.

"I am going to attend Mass. Would like to join me?" I asked.

"Yes, I would like to," she said.

Walking into the little side chapel, we saw many of our friends. We smiled at one another. Being in church brings a sense of togetherness for everyone. This is special. We do not see each other all the time, but when we do, we recognize one another. This is part of the Camino—the Way.

After Mass, my friend and I went to a restaurant. We shared a lovely meal, including dessert. The restaurant gave us a discount because we are pilgrims. This is splendid. I guess I could say being a pilgrim has its little perks. We were not in a hurry to get back to the albergue. The moon and stars shined on Burgos tonight. The cathedral is lit up so beautifully. It is simply divine.

Reaching the albergue, my friend and I said, "Good night." We wished each other a pleasant day tomorrow.

I crawled into my bunk. I am filled with gratitude. Starting out today, I walked in the wrong direction. A couple helped me get on the right path. Feeling the closeness of the divine then falling on my knees. Seeing three crosses made today extra special. Connecting with two lovely women who walked with me through the city, took me to the pharmacy, and we found our albergue. Uniting with friends at Mass at the cathedral brought today to a close.

This I know for sure, I am not alone on this journey. I share this with everyone I come into contact with.

Day 14 ~ Hontanas

Inspiration

In the morning, it was easy to leave Burgos. The albergue is at the end of the city. Passing through El Parral Park and Hospital del Rey, I came to a roadway. Finding the markings will not be a problem. The walkway is paved. This will take me out to the wooded area of Burgos. There is no rocky terrain for now.

As dawn peeked through, the sun's heat became unbearable. I reached into my pocket and took out my washcloth. After wetting it, I wrapped it around my neck as a choker. Although the path is tolerable, the scourging heat is getting to me. I became restless. At this point, I wanted to leave everything behind. No rucksack, no jacket, no stick, nothing at all. Feeling uncomfortable is just horrible. If I took everything off and left it behind what will I have left.

"This is it! I do not want to do this anymore. I simply cannot go on. This heat is excruciating," I shouted. "Stop and look around," I screamed.

Then my feelings became highly emotional. Streams of tears rolled down my face. "I am trying hard to do this. This heat is too much for me," I said to myself.

"You are trying too hard. Take it slowly and do not give up," a little voice whispered.

At that moment, I wiped my face. I stopped to see where I was. All I could see were plains and hills. This seemed to only make it hotter. After a while, I picked up my feet and began walking again.

There is no one in sight. I am alone. All I can see is a stretch of land around me. I did not look up at the sky. I glared at the ground. As I walked, I hung my head. Then a gentle wind touched my cheek.

"Do not give up. I am with you," the little voice said softly.

Hearing these words, I repeated it over and over again. This calmed me. It kept me focused on hiking.

Then I remembered Psalm 27:1,

> The Lord is my light and my salvation; whom shall I fear?
> The Lord is the stronghold of my life; of whom shall I be afraid?

I need to make myself strong to walk this journey. Today, there are no peaks or mountains to climb only hills and valleys. I am not afraid of being in the wilderness. The heat makes me think I cannot do this.

Inspiration

Passing through Rabé de las Calzadas, I am on my way to Hornillos del Camino. Taking out bread and fruit from my jacket, I ate my morning snack. This seemed to be the hottest day to date. As good fortune would have it, I came to a riverbed. The water looked so refreshing. As much as I wanted to stay, I needed to set out again. It is still morning. I did not want to lag further behind. It will become hotter as the day progresses.

Between the San Bol River and Hontanas, I saw a woman with a baby stroller and a little girl about four years old. They came out from a side trail. When I came up to them, the little girl looked at me. She was dressed in a flowery summer dress with a hat. Her big brown eyes sparkled.

"Buen Camino," she said with a smile.

"Buen Camino to you, sweetie," I replied.

I stopped to look at the woman and her children. In this blistering heat, a mother and her children are here. I am not picturing this correctly in my mind.

"Are you walking the Camino?" I asked the woman.

"Yes, we are. My husband is back there and he will join us soon. We have been walking at least two months," she replied with a smile. I looked down the narrow trail and I saw a man approaching us.

"Good-bye. I wish you all the best," the woman said in joy.

"Take care. Buen Camino," I answered. We smiled and nodded our heads.

I walked away thinking this is amazing. A father, a mother, and their children are walking the Camino. A flow of energy went through my body. "Yes, I can do it," I whispered. This gave me new hope.

On my way to Hontanas, I met a couple. They also decided to stop and stay at Hontanas. Folks mentioned when we reach Hontanas, we would have walked 300 kilometers. This is good news. We will have another 500 kilometers to go. I felt relieved at the thought of walking almost half the way.

Walking to Hontanas is like entering into a bowl. I kept this thought in the back of my mind. It seemed as if there is no end in sight on this trail. It continued twisting and turning until it led to Hontanas. The rocky terrain is steep as I walked. Descending became interesting. I tried hard not to fall or strain my feet and knees. Then I remembered the bowl. I set one foot in front of the other going down these crooked turns. By noon, I reached the village. I had walked thirty kilometers.

The village is quaint. There is not much to see or do here. I can see why. It took every bit of strength in my being to bring me here today. Reaching here is a remarkable feat. Today's walk seemed to be the longest day so far. The temperature exceeded anything so far. I could not walk beyond Hontanas. Going another eight kilometers to Castrojeriz would be too much for me today.

Inspiration

Strolling towards the albergue seemed to help the heat evaporate. I checked in and then found my cot for the night. I decided to wash clothes before showering. This albergue provides laundry baskets. I filled up the basket with water. As I put my dirty clothes in the basket, I felt the urge to get in the basket. When I got in the basket, I began to stomp on my clothes. The water was cold and invigorating to my feet and legs. Its coolness went all through my exhausted body. A few other women picked up their baskets and joined me. Before we knew it, almost everyone brought their baskets to the grass. Our stomping turned into a dancing fest that alleviated our sweat and dirt from today. With joy, we celebrated one of the hottest days. After soaking, stomping, and dancing, our clothes are ready for hanging. There are many clotheslines on the side of the albergue. Then I scooted myself over to the showers.

Feeling refreshed, I came outside to sit on the porch. I applied my anti-inflammatory cream to my knees and feet. This feels soothing. Before I sleep tonight, I will ice my knees. Staring at my feet, I came to realize how important my feet are to me. My feet are in their worst shape now. If I make it to the end of this journey, I promised myself I will not neglect my feet again. They are simply too precious. I will take better care of my feet from now on.

In no time, I could see some of my friends walking into Hontanas. A couple from Italy sat down to eat their lunch.

"Do you want to walk with us to Castrojeriz?" they asked me.

"Thank you, but I will stay here tonight. Today has been a little too hot for me. I need to rest. My feet and knees are hurting," I replied.

We chatted for a bit longer until they felt it was time for them to leave. We stood up and hugged each other.

"Buen Camino," I said to them. They picked up their rucksacks and started to walk. They looked back at me and blew kisses in the air. I did the same.

"I hope to see you again," I said softly.

As I was standing, I looked around the tiny village. I did not see a church. If there is no church, there will be no Mass. I felt a little moved by this. Well, it is nap time. When I reached my cot, I could hear all kinds of snoring. It sounded like trains going in and out of stations.

"My nap time will not be here," I said softly. I took out my rolled up sleeping bag and I went back to the porch. Standing outside, I could see a little tree with shade. "There is where I will nap for today," I whispered. I rolled out the sleeping bag and laid on it. Although there is no wind, I have shade. Closing my eyes, I imagined a breeze covering my head and body. I fell asleep.

Inspiration

Waking up to sounds, I looked around to see where it was coming from. A group of pilgrims walked in the albergue to check-in. They are unhappy because the albergue is full. Feeling disappointed, the group sat for a little while. Then they got up and started to walk to another village. Will there be beds for them at the next place? This is a question in the back of every hiker's mind. Some folks have opted to sleep under the moon and stars. The weather is nice at night so this makes it convenient.

As the day came to an end, it became a little cooler. It is dinner time. The albergue provides a little dining area to eat. Paying a pilgrim's price, the meal will be homemade and filling. As I walked back to my cot, I noticed many of the folks were up and out of the room. Aha, they are on their way to dinner. I will join the group. Making my way to the dining area, I saw some friends.

"Could you sit with us tonight?" a friend asked me.

"Sure, I will be more than glad to," I answered.

We found a table. Six of us sat down and talked about our happenings today. Someone asked the group if anyone saw a man, a woman, and young children today.

"Yes, I did. I thought that was amazing. This family gave me hope and inspiration to walk today. Just before running into the couple, I was ready to leave everything behind and give up," I said.

"Yes, this couple also gave me the energy to continue," another friend replied.

We were all in agreement the couple and children saved us today.

My dinner was simply divine. A delicious salad and potatoes filled my empty belly. After dinner, we were enchanted by lovely music. The evening is perfect.

"After today's heartaches and heat, who would have imagine tonight would be so pleasant?" I said. We all laughed.

"This is absolutely true," a friend replied.

Then the musicians came to our table. We listened in delight. We kept quiet and enjoyed the melody. After dinner, we made our way back to our room to sleep for the night. I picked up ice for my knees.

In the back of my mind, I wondered about the family I saw earlier during the day. Where are they now? Where will they stay tonight? These were some of the questions I thought about. This family gave me hope and inspiration to reach Hontanas. The family instilled life into me when I felt miserable. Thinking I could not go on any longer, there they were in front of my eyes. I pray wherever they are they will find peace and comfort tonight. Little do they know they inspired many hikers on the walk today.

Inspiration

Sweltering heat did not make it easy. Giving up the entire hike today would have been the easiest thing to do.

"Do not give up. I am with you," my inner voice whispered.

"I am thankful I did not give up today," I whispered. The soft gentle voice inside me keeps me treading along.

Day 15 ~ Boadilla del Camino

Encounter

I live for another day. Getting up early in the morning, I am on my way to Castrojeriz. The morning dew in Hontanas gives me a get-up-and-go motivation for today. Breathing in clean air clears my mind. I am ready for hiking today. As I begin to move, I can see little lights in the distance. Hikers are all ready for the journey. Although I am may not be with them, I know now that I am not walking alone.

After trekking about eight kilometers, I can see a fortress on a hill. The villagers live below the castle. I have reached Castrojeriz. Trees are terraced on the hillside giving life to this old tiny community. The morning light gives an array of color to this tiny village. It wakes up to a new dawn. This village has little shops. The famous collegiate church, La Virgen del Manzano, welcomes pilgrims into the town. This church goes back to the ninth century. In this church, a famous statue of Saint James the Pilgrim is displayed.

He stands wearing a three-cornered hat, holding a staff in his right hand, he is carrying a gourd, and carved shells cover him. As I continued walking, I came to another little town. The curvy pathway began to lead me out of the area. Passing two little houses with flowery yards and short wooden fences, I could see a middle age man in the distance. He was sitting in a rocking chair on his porch. Wearing no shirt only a light blue cutoff jeans, I could see he was soaking in the marvelous sunshine. As I passed him, he jumped out of his chair.

"Are your walking this road to Santiago de Compostela?" he asked politely.

"Yes, I am," I smiled at the man.

He walked to his gate and swung it open. I stopped walking. He immediately came up to me and grabbed my shoulders tightly. I froze like an ice cube.

"What is this man trying to do to me?" I whispered quietly. He looked into my eyes, picked me off the ground, and leaned over me.

"I am going to give you something to take with you," he said. Then he kissed me on the cheek. Wow! Instantly, I felt electricity flowing throughout my body.

"Buen Camino," he shouted. With his strong hands, he pulled me away from him and put me back on the ground. I thought I would never touch ground again, but I did. My legs felt like spaghetti noodles. I could barely stand up. The man held me firm so that I would not fall. I was stunned by this experience.

"What did I do to deserve this kiss? Never in my wildest dreams would I have imagined a kiss. This caught me off guard. What do I do now?" I said in amazement. I looked at the man and smiled. "This cannot be happening to me. I am dreaming," I said softly. Then I pinched myself. This is real. A man kissed me. I started to shake. "Thank you for your kind wishes," I said to the man.

Slowly, I turned and walked down the path. Then I stopped and turned around to see if he was still there. Yes, he is standing and leaning against the fence. Then he raised his arm and waved to me. I waved back at him. Holding my cheek, I turned and continued walking. I kept silent for a while.

Two weeks into this journey, I would have never imagined something like this. This is surprising. I reached for my camelbak and drank water to relieve my excitement. I needed to cool off. After thinking about it a little more, I realized this is meant to be. I could not explain it. Whatever it is, there is a reason.

Under the blazing heat, I crossed over the Pisuerga River. Walking across the Itero Bridge, an eleven-arched stone bridge gave me comfort. I felt as if I was climbing up to heaven. Counting every arched stone brought calmness inside me. Making my way to the middle of the long bridge, I had a sense I was leaving behind Burgos and entering into the region of Palencia. Pisuerga River borders between these two areas. Standing on the bridge gave me strength. This is one of the longest bridges on the trail. I can see small hills ahead. Staring back, I leave behind Burgos. There are few trees around. A little ways down the path, it became rocky and staggering.

In a distance, I could see a trail of dust. I came to a halt. I took out my cloth and washed my face. I cleaned my eyes. "What is up ahead? What could it be?" I asked myself.

As it came closer, I could see a donkey, a dog, a man with a long stick, and a herd of sheep. It is a man herding his sheep. The ground is dry and the herd is kicking up dust. I stopped to let the parade pass by.

I could see the donkey leading the procession. As I looked at the donkey, it looked back at me. I did not move. The donkey stopped and looked fiercely at me. I remained calm.

"Do not move. Be still," I said in a shivering voice.

The donkey walked over to me. I looked to see where the sheepherder was. Looking at the donkey, my eyes were filled with tears. My tears flowed like a gushing dam. I puckered my lips and trembled. "What are you going to do with me?" I cried. The donkey winked at me with one of his big brown eyes. "No. This cannot be happening to me. A donkey is winking his eye at me," I said in a low voice. "What is happening? What is going on with me today?" I sighed.

Before I could think about what else to say, I heard the dog barking. "Oh no a donkey who winks and a barking dog is in the act. What is going on here?" I asked.

I turned away from the donkey and I could see the dog rapidly approaching me. I stood guard with my stick in case the dog decided to attack me. Lo and behold, the dog barked at the donkey. Immediately, the donkey walked over to the other side of the dirt road.

The sheepherder was close by herding about thirty sheep. Walking in the middle of the road, the herder wore a hat and carried a stick. Looking tired, he could see what had happened to me. Mumbling under his breath, the donkey continued walking. The dog stopped barking. The sheep have the right-of-way.

I moved a few steps off the dirt road alongside a grassy area. In no time, the sheep walked passed me kicking up dust. I could smell and taste the dust. By this time, the sheep were baaing at me. Holding my breath was probably the best thing to do. With all the sheep passing by, I could hold my breath only for a little while and then release it. I covered my mouth. As the dust settled, I began to walk again.

I could see hikers from a distance. "I wonder if they bumped into this herd of sheep. This is too funny. I am saying this now, but at the time, I was scared. I did not know what to expect," I said with laughter.

With all that has occurred today, I still have the oomph to do what I need to do. I need to walk nine more kilometers to Boadilla del Camino. It will be a good stop for today.

As I walked into Boadilla del Camino, I heard church bells. It is midday. I walked a little ways and passed an albergue. Then I stopped and made a U-turn. I walked back to the albergue. This is where I will spend the night. The albergue had opened and I checked in. I could not believe my eyes. This albergue has single rooms for pilgrims. This is perfect. I need a room tonight with four walls and a door.

After showering, I walked out of my room and saw two friends from Korea. It has been over a week since I last saw these women. We were hungry. Since the albergue has a restaurant, we talked a little while and shared a meal together. Gathering with folks works out well, especially after a grueling day.

After our meal, I walked outside around to the back of the albergue. I saw a beautiful tree with long branches. It had a shady area. I walked over to the tree and sat down. In the snap of a finger, I took a snooze. I awoke feeling rain or something wet on my head.

Encounter

Rubbing my hair to see what it was I could not believe what I saw.

"No, No, No. I just washed my hair," I said loudly. It is bird droppings. "My luck, what else is going to happen to me today?" I asked myself. I got up, went back into the albergue, and took another shower. Since hiking, I have not taken two showers in a day. Today is a first.

Now I have the energy to go into the little village. As I was walking, I passed by old wooden dovecots. These dovecots are built so that doves could use them to build their nests. Boadilla del Camino has many fields and doves help the farmers. These birds would help eat the insects and they also made a tasty meal.

"Hum, I wondered if the bird droppings I had earlier could have been from a dove," I said curiously. "Of course, I will never know this because I did not see a bird. I felt it only that it came from the sky," I chuckled.

As I walked into this tenth century village, I could see the oldness. I found a little place where I could pick up fruit and bread. Few folks live here. In its prime, Boadilla del Camino provided services for the pilgrims. The village had a hospital, a monastery, and several churches.

Standing in the middle of the town square, I saw the church of La Asunción. In the church, there is a fourteenth-century baptismal font. This font is carved from a single stone. The circular-shaped baptismal font stands on a solid pillar supported by twelve columns.

141

The carvings are unique. The artwork portrays flowers, crosses, and arches. Outside the church in the town square, is a fifteenth-century Gothic pillory. This pillory was use for public executions for serious crimes. As I walked over to it, I touched the column. I wondered how many criminals were executed here. I stood there for a moment in silence and prayer.

Feeling worn out, I walked back to the albergue. I stayed in my room. I began to think about my family. Just think in nine months, I will be moving back home. Joy came over me. I will be enjoying my family and friends again. This is such a good feeling. All I need to do now is finish this walk. Then I will rejoice fully.

Reflecting back on today's events made me realized I am blessed. From a kiss, to a donkey who winks, a sheepherder, a barking dog, and a herd of sheep were my highlights today. I would have never expected such excitement on this journey. Then to walk into Boadilla del Camino made it a splendid day.

Now I can see why folks walking the Camino have their own stories. Every story is unique. I see and experience this journey differently day after day. Each traveler experiences something different along the way. At the same time, we look out for one another.

The Camino is teaching me to be filled with hope and anticipation for the next day. The encounters are teaching tools for me.

Enlightened

After sleeping one night alone in a room all by myself, I am beginning to appreciate this walk more than ever. It amazes me how one night could make a difference. This morning I feel something different. There is something more to this walk than the experience. Taking three deep breaths before getting out of bed to begin my walk to Carrión de los Condes, I felt fresh and alive.

"This is the beginning of a new day for the rest of my life," I thought to myself.

I put on my jacket. It felt a little heavy this morning because I put a piece of bread, dates and an orange for the day's adventure into my pocket. I folded my sleeping bag and tucked it in the bottom of my rucksack.

Quietly, I put on my hat and carried my rucksack and stick. I tiptoed outside the albergue. This way I would not awaken anyone else. I noticed five Italian young men leaving to get a head start. Then a friend from Italy was also up early. As I was putting on my shoes, she passed by.

"Good morning," she said quietly.

"Good morning and Buen Camino," I replied.

Then she turned and whispered, "Buen Camino."

After tying my shoes, I stood up and took a deep breath. "Today is going to be one of the best days yet," I said. The ground was wet. It rained last night. This will be fine. Maybe it will be cooler to walk today.

Then I heard something. "Could I be imagining things? Is it the sound of thunder?" I asked myself. Then I saw lightning in a distance. The rain became heavier. I reached for my poncho in the bottom of my rucksack and slipped it over my head. I am ready for the weather.

As I continued walking, I noticed the light in my flashlight was fading in and out. "Of all mornings, this cannot be happening. Why now?" I whispered. I promised myself as soon as I reach Carrión de los Condes I will buy new batteries.

Walking along I kept shaking the flashlight hoping that it would not go out. I remembered an old saying; *the early bird catches the worm*. In this case, the early bird will not catch the worm if it does not know where it is going. I looked ahead and I saw a little sparkle of light. I could not figure out the distance between the light and myself because it was so dark. There is no need to be frightened. Someone is up ahead. Despite my efforts my flashlight went out!

"Great. Now what do I do?" I thought. I called out to the hiker ahead to see if he or she could share their light.

"Hello, do you have a flashlight? I said aloud. Once again, I repeated myself. The third time I shouted. Then I faintly heard a voice.

"Yes, I have a flashlight," someone answered.

"Please wait. My flashlight is out. I am walking in darkness. Wait for me please," I said.

"I will wait for you," the voice replied.

By this time, the rain had gotten heavier. The thunder and lightning were louder and clearer. When I approached the light, it was my friend from Italy.

"Thank you so much," I said to her.

"No worries. We will walk together," she said.

"Are we walking in the direction of the wind, rain, thunder, and lightning?" I asked.

"It looks like it," she replied.

The thunder pounded its way across the sky. The lightning kept getting closer and closer to us. Two times the lightning seemed to come between my friend and me. We barely could walk by now. The rain is blowing in all directions. Tall trees are swaying in a circle.

Suddenly, the lightning struck a third time. This time I fell to the ground. It hit so hard I lost my eyesight.

My hair on my body stood up. The back of my neck pulled tightly. I could not see.

"Where are you? I cannot see," I shouted. "Stop, please do not leave me," I called out.

Then I heard my friend say quietly, "I am standing in front of you. I will not leave you."

"I cannot see. I think the lightning was too strong," I began to explain. At this point, I squinted. I could see little lights in both eyes. I squinted more. These lights look like stars.

As I was squinting, I thought of the conversion of Saul who was struck by lightning. In Acts 9:3-6, Saul made threats of murder against the disciples.

> Now as he was going along and approaching Damascus, suddenly a light from heaven flashed around him. He fell to the ground and heard a voice saying to him, "Saul, Saul, why do you persecute me?" He asked, "Who are you, Lord?" The reply came, "I am Jesus, whom you are persecuting. But get up and enter the city, and you will be told what you are to do."

As the Biblical story continues, Saul becomes the Apostle Paul.

Then I felt a hand on my shoulder. It is my friend. "Are you fine?" she asked.

Enlightened

As I kept squinting, I could see a dark figure in front of me. The little lights began to go away. My hair on my body relaxed. The pain in my neck subsided. My vision became clearer. I do not know how long it was before I could see again. Wind and rain continued. My friend and I hugged each other tightly. We did not speak. Then silence. After a while, we relaxed and looked at each other and smiled. It rained heavily on us.

"I can see you. Do we continue?" I asked.

"Yes, but slowly. I have my flashlight. Stay close to me," she said calmly. We put one foot in front of the other and started to walk again.

"I think we walked through the eye of this storm," I said quietly.

"Yes, we did. Stay close by. I do not want to lose you," she responded.

Before long, we were standing on a hill. We needed to go down the hill to continue our walk. Daybreak was peeking through already. Since my friend had the flashlight, she ran down the slippery hill first. All I could see was a lot of water and mud all around.

"This is going to be a slippery slide for me. Please shine your flashlight on the hill," I asked. She turned around and flashed the light. Now, it is my turn. As I ran down the hill, I looked over to the side. All I could see was a big drop all the way down. It looked like a dark bottomless pit. I did not want to go there. Getting down to the bottom of the hill, I ran into my friend. She grabbed me.

"We made it," she shouted.

"Yes, we did," I yelled.

We took deep breaths and walked on. I am so thankful for God and my friend this morning. We experienced the worst of this storm. Walking out of the storm is unbelievable.

As Saul experienced his conversion, I think my friend and I encountered something worth sharing about to others one day.

Daylight is everywhere now. The rain continued, but with little wind. My friend and I looked behind us. We could see the storm heading in the direction of other hikers. At least, they will be able to see where they are going. They have sunlight; no darkness.

In the distance, we could see the town of Frómista. The town is bigger than other villages in this area. It has flat terrain and surrounded by a lot of wheat. My friend and I decided to take a break in the town. We found a few churches in Frómista. Many pilgrims would stop and go in to visit the San Martin Church. This church has one of the best architectural designs. Its simplicity is very much like a little castle with two towers.

As I left Frómista, I could feel my energy picking up again. Heading toward Carrión de los Condes, will be a slow gradual hike. Walking along the path, trees gave shade to the trail. The trail was wet and muddy. This does not matter after experiencing the storm this morning. I could hear bells. As I turned around, I could see cyclists. I moved to the side of the trail to let them whiz by. The cyclists passed by saying, "Buen Camino."

"Buen Camino," my friend said out loud.

I waved to them as they rode away. These cyclists were covered with mud. Aha, they also went through the storm.

Once we reached Población de Campos, the road split. Going to the right would take us to the village of Villovieco. We decided to pass through the commonly used route to Revenga de Campos, Villarmentero de Campos, and Villalcázar de Sirga heading to Carrión de los Condes. The rest of the way turned out to be good in light of natural forces this morning.

Carrión de los Condes is an agriculture area known for wheat, wine, and all kinds of produce. Walking into Carrión de los Condes, the center of the town is the Santa Maria del Camino Church. On the side of the church is the albergue. Our rucksacks were one of the first in line. We needed to wait for the albergue to open. Walking around the corner, we walked to the church. The doorway of the church is an eye catcher. The exquisite artwork is carved above the doorway. Entering into the church, we sat in silence. After a while, I got up and walked outside. I walked over to a store and bought batteries for my flashlight. I am ready for tomorrow's journey.

From a distance, I could see friends walking into the town. As they got closer, several friends came over to me and chatted. "We are glad to see you. After hearing about the storm, we waited a while before walking. We thought about you, especially walking in today's storm," they said with concern.

"Thank you for thinking about me, but there is another friend. We are here now and that is all what matters. It was quite an experience this morning," I replied. Then we made our way around the corner to get in line.

It did not take too long, the albergue opened. As our credentials were stamped, a nun walked each person up a spiral stairway to their bed. My friend and I were taken to different beds. We waved to each other. After showering, I iced my knee and napped for a while.

Before I opened my eyes, I heard laughter. I got up. All the beds are filled with rucksacks. Everyone has arrived. I freshen up and walked downstairs. Many friends are listening to music sung by the nuns. The music set the pace for the evening. One of the nuns played a guitar. This is a treat. Then we were invited to have a meal.

After our meal, we attended Mass. The priest blessed the pilgrims. Then we rejoined our gathering again. One of the nuns asked if there is anyone musical to play the guitar. One of my friends played the guitar and another played the flute. The evening set harmony and peace. We sat on the spiral stairway and on the floor. Many of us sat in silence listening to the breathtaking sounds.

What started out today ended in splendor for everyone. We experienced probably one of the worst events with this morning's storm. On this journey, we do not know what lies ahead. We can only have faith and trust in one another and our God.

I experienced a conversion today. Something I would have never expected. With today's events, it prepared me better to do this walk. My hope to continue will be entirely up to me now. I need to find the determination to complete it. After today, I have found the willpower to finish. The strength and courage is instilled in me.

Day 17 ~ Terradillos de los Templarios

Serenity

After yesterday's experience, my flashlight and extra batteries are set and ready for today's journey. I am hoping for beautiful weather. My goal today is to walk to Sahagún. If I do not make it that far, at least to Terradillos de los Templarios. Many hikers are walking to Sahagún. It will be a long day, at least thirty-eight kilometers. Although I would like to walk the distance, it will depend on how I feel.

Making my way out of Carrión de los Condes, I could smell fresh bread. The aroma went into my nostrils. I would like a piece of warm, fresh baked bread with a bit of butter. I savored the thought of eating the bread. As I continued walking, the scent stayed with me until I was out of the village. This is a nice send off to begin my daily journey. I reached into my pocket and took out a piece of my stale bread from yesterday.

I pretended this piece of bread was much like the freshness I am experiencing this morning.

As I crossed the Carrión River, I came to the San Zoilo Monastery. This monastery dates back to the tenth century and was of importance in the Castilian region. The cloister architecture shows tall rounded concrete arches which dates back to the tenth and eleventh century. Resting for a little while, I could imagine the hospitality within this monastery. Back then several hospices were around the Carrión area. Many pilgrims passed through and perhaps stayed here as well. What is truly amazing is that some of these ancient buildings are still standing along the path. History lives on and the buildings speak for themselves.

The terrain is flat. Although there are not many trees, the beauty of the grain fields is inspiring. The different earth-tone shades cover the fields. The slight breeze sweeps through like a wave, as it gently touches the tips of the meadow. As sunlight reaches ground, shades of various colors appear on the path. Depending on the sun, sky, and terrain, different shades of color appear in this area.

Today is cooler. Crossing over irrigation canals, the water is soothing and brings a chill down my back. As I drink water from my camelbak, I give thanks for this beautiful day. The nice breeze and mild sun keep the temperature cool. The chirping of the birds brings a graceful sound as I stroll down a pathway.

To my surprise, I see a couple sitting and hugging off to the side of the road. It is lovely to behold. The feeling of serenity is not only for me. As I walked past the couple, the gentleman turned his head to look back. Seeing me, he smiled.

"Buen Camino," I said. He replied the same. The woman looked at me and smiled. I nodded my head and waved to them.

"Hello. How are you?" she asked.

"I am doing fine. This is a beautiful day," I replied. "You look familiar. I think I met you last week in another village."

"That is right. We are engaged. Doing this walk is our test for each other. We are hoping to complete it together," the gentleman said.

"Yes, I can see this is a challenge not only for couples to do, but for everyone," I answered. We wished each other a pleasant day and I continued on my way.

At mid-morning crossing over the Cañada Real stream, I could see from a distance the church bell tower of Calzadilla de la Cueza. The tiny village is nearby. Picking up my feet, I marched into the community. I needed to go and relieve myself, so I looked around and saw a bar. Dashing inside, I saw some folks having a morning snack.

"Buen Camino," someone said. Without answering, I hurriedly looked around to see where the restrooms were. Then I saw the sign. Running into the restroom, I relieved myself. As I came out, I saw a group of friends.

"Buen Camino. Sorry, but I needed to go to the restroom," I replied.

They laughed and offered me a seat.

"Thank you, but I need to keep walking. After all, I am a tortoise. If I sit down now, I do not think I will be able to finish my walk today," I joked. Waving to the group, I walked out the door and headed down the roadway.

My knee began to ache. "Hmmm, will I make it to Sahagún today?" I asked myself. For now I will continue and then decide later if I shall continue or stop.

After leaving Calzadilla de la Cueza, I came to several routes to choose from. I could continue along the pathway or fork off to the left into a forested area. The other choice would be following a path along a river and going onto a side road. I decided to stay on the main roadway. I am hoping other folks will be walking the same way. By going this way, it will be a straight shot instead of going into the forest or along the river path. Before long, I could see walkers up ahead.

"Yes. Taking this shorter route will make a difference in my journey today," I said with glee.

Soon, however, the ache in my knee increased. I had only my walking stick to depend upon. At this point, I decided not to walk all the way to Sahagún. I do not know where I am going to stay for the night, but I knew the condition of my knee made it necessary for me to find an alternative place to stop.

As I walked into the town of Santa Maria de las Tiendas, I felt a little relief. Seeing familiar faces sitting outside a little building brought joy to me. Forgetting about my knee, I hobbled my way over to meet up with the group.

"You are here," someone said.

"Yes, I am here with an aching knee," I replied. I reached into my jacket and pulled out my anti-inflammatory ointment. Rubbing the ointment on my knee, I could feel some relief.

"When you are done with your ointment, could I use it for my knee?" one of my friends asked.

"Here it is," I said. She smiled and thanked me.

"How far are you walking today?" she asked.

"Looks like I am going as far as Terradillos de los Templarios. At least, I would have walked more than halfway to Sahagún," I answered.

"Could I walk with you? I do not know if I will stop at Terradillos de los Templarios or walk further," she asked.

"Of course, I will be delighted to have the company," I responded.

She gave me back the ointment. We looked at each other with mutual determination, picked ourselves up, and started to walk.

Terradillos de los Templarios would be the next town. We walked through a shaded area. The ground was flat and partially paved in certain places. In all, I could not ask for a better day to walk. With our knees hurting, we took it slowly step by step. My friend and I chatted and laughed along the way. We were a good distraction for one another. At this point, we were in no rush for a fast pace. Sometimes slow is better. Although it may take a little longer, in the end we will get there. After a while, we reached our destination.

As we entered into Terradillos de los Templarios, we saw many of our friends. Some were staying for the night. Others were taking a break then walking onto Sahagún. I felt this is where I needed to stay for the night. After finding the albergue, I chose to rest my knee for tomorrow's trekking. My friend decided to continue walking. We hugged each other. Then she headed off.

After showering and washing clothes, I went to my bunk to take a snooze. I was grateful for how pleasant this day was, despite the increased pain in my knee. I applied an ice pack to my knee and fell asleep.

I awoke to the delicious aroma of food.

"Where is the smell coming from? Who is cooking? Is it dinner time already?" I asked myself. Looking at my watch, I had slept for a good while. Looking around, there was still sunlight. Napping has always been an important part of this journey. If someone were to ask me what did you do on this pilgrimage? I would simply say, "Eat, Sleep, and Walk."

Feeling refreshed, my nose followed the wonderful smell of something good to eat. To my surprise, a group of friends were cooking pasta, pomodoro sauce, and tossed salad. This is what I smell.

"Hello," my friends said in awe.

"Hi everyone. I am glad to see you," I replied.

"Please come and join us," a friend suggested.

"Thank you," I said in delight.

They made a place for me to sit and join them. Perfect! Then I thought this is so sweet. On a journey like this, friends do take care of friends. We all come from different parts of the world; however, we have the same basic needs—eat, sleep, and walk.

After dinner, I helped with washing and cleaning up. Then one of our friends began to play the flute. Another friend played his guitar. We sat as a group and enjoyed the beautiful music. Some folks shared their stories of today's events. Others shared their life stories. Then one of the women began to sob.

"Why are you crying?" someone asked her.

"I did not know I would make it this far walking the Camino," she said.

We all looked at each other and nodded to one another. Yes, we could all relate to this so well. We kept silent for a little while then some of us stood up and walked over to her and hugged her. Before we knew it, everyone got up and hugged each other. We are thankful and most of all grateful to be here with good friends. We shared more of our stories. These stories may not all be the same, but there are similarities. I guess this is what makes this walk unique and challenging and what bonds us.

Making my way back to my bunk to turn in for the night, I detoured outside the albergue. I looked up at the sky to see the stars. The night is gorgeous. Stars are shining brightly. Everything is still and dark. I could smell a sweet fragrance in the air. I looked around to see if there was anyone outside besides me. I was alone. Closing my eyes, I breathed in the delicate scent. After a while, I felt relaxed.

"Do I want to go inside to sleep or stay outside?" I asked myself. "I am enjoying this beautiful evening," I said. Then I heard a dog bark.

"I think the dog has answered my question," I said with amusement.

Crawling in bed, I took three deep breaths. Between each breath, I reflected on today's walk. "No, I did not make it to Sahagún. I am not in it as a race because there is no contest," I said softly.

Many friends will end at Sahagún and return back to their countries from there. They have a schedule to keep. I do not. I have time. I will take all the time I need to finish this walk.

"I am in no rush to finish," I whispered.

This journey started as an impossible dream and it is becoming a reality for me. Although I hurt and experience pain, nonetheless days like today bring peace, comfort, and joy to a seeker. I am a pilgrim seeking an impossible dream. Taking one day at a time from sunrise to sunset carries me to reach my goal. Along the way, I meet wonderful and interesting folks from different places and different walks of life. Walking into the ancient towns and villages inspires me to continue. Not knowing what is up ahead, but looking for a shell shaped marker to guide me upon the path. The weather is unpredictable. Yesterday's chaotic weather is a complete opposite of today's beauty. Tomorrow is a mystery, but at the end of the day I will have a story to share.

There is quiet and silence now.

Day 18 ~ El Burgo Ranero

Rivers

Getting up this morning is simply breathtaking. Some of the folks walking were beginning early as well. As I filled my camelbak, the cool water feels good. Bringing the camelbak hose through the hole of my rucksack and resting it on my shoulder and against my neck helped to keep me cool. After tying my shoe laces, I stood up, put on my hat and grabbed my walking stick.

"I am ready for today's adventure," I said raring to go.

Stepping outside of the albergue I looked left then right. It is dark, but I could hear sounds. I heard laughter and chatter from folks. Turning on my flashlight, I began to walk. Before I could see what was in front of me, I heard someone say, "Hello." I stopped.

Then two people looked at me. "Could we join you this morning?" one of them asked.

"Of course, this morning is too beautiful to be walking alone," I answered.

Leaving the village, we kept quiet for a while. This morning we seem to keep to our own thoughts. We are not in a hurry, although I am lagging behind. I could smell the green pine trees. They are tall and strong. Their trunks are thick, round, and knotted. Considering the size of the knots, they look old. Then I heard a sound.

"Bridge up ahead. Be careful," someone said.

"Be not afraid. You can do this," a little voice inside me whispered.

As I came to the bridge, I could see two lights on the other side. Then I heard running water. This is the Templarios River. Although it is still dark, I wondered how deep and wide this river is. I do not know if I should stop here and not cross it. I pulled myself together.

"Where are you? Are you crossing the bridge?" someone said aloud.

"I am at the bridge about to cross it," I responded. I started to walk across. I could not look down to see what was below because it was too dark. Making my way across, I could feel the bridge swaying from side to side. "Could this be my imagination?" I said aloud. The wind started to pick up as I continued walking.

"Be not afraid. I am with you," the voice whispered again.

"If it is you, Lord, I am in your hands. Please do not let me trip or fall," I said trembling. I could feel the bridge pulling downward to the center. The cold mist from the water touched my face. The freshness brought tingles to my entire body. At this point, I could see large rocks on both sides of the bridge.

"Wow! This is very close to the water under the bridge," I said aloud. Picking up my feet, I quickly walked the rest of the way.

Before reaching the other side, I felt as if I was walking uphill. The bridge is arced upward now. How enchanting and exciting to experience something this early in the morning, but I really need to get to the other side quickly. Finally, I could see the river bank, and realized the other side is near.

"Thank you, Lord, for bringing me across this river," I whispered. Then I took a deep breath.

"I made it across," I said gratefully.

"Yes, you did it. Now, let us finish the rest of the way," a friend said.

At daybreak, we walked into the village of Moratinos. This quaint place has one roadway. After seeing the yellow shell marker, we were leaving the village. San Nicholás del Real Camino is the next town. It is about two more kilometers from here.

By this time, I was hungry. I reached into my pocket for a piece of fruit. I took out an orange. As I peeled it, the juices squirted into my face. The fresh fragrance went up into my nostrils.

"I am an orange today. This is going to be delicious," I said to myself. As I shared the orange with my friends, they thanked me. "This is juicy and sweet," I said softly. I could hear my friends saying the same thing. "Food is especially tasty at a time like this," I answered back.

Today is a beautiful day for walking. By mid-morning, my friends and I reached San Nicholás del Real Camino. This is the last part of the Camino trail in the Palencia region. After this region, it will be León.

I refilled my camelbak with water. My friends decided to stay a little longer, but I was eager to continue, so I picked up my rucksack and started to walk again.

"Buen Camino. Thank you for this morning's walk together," I said and smiled.

"Buen Camino. We will see you later," they replied.

As I walked a little ways, I came to a second bridge. I will cross the Sequillo River. Before I began, I took a deep breath in and exhaled equally. I want to find my balance while crossing this bridge. Inhale and exhale equally. It feels different. Taking each step to the rhythm makes a difference in my walking. I stopped for a little bit to see the river flow. The water looks clean, cold, and refreshing. Touching the side of the bridge I feel tempted to jump into the river, but I realized that if

I were to jump in the water I would not finish my journey today.

"Do I want to do this?" I asked myself.

"No, do not jump into the river," my inner voice said.

Instantly, I made my way to the center of the bridge and stayed there. Picking up my breathing rhythm again helped me to finish the crossing. This makes me feel balanced and in rhythm.

From the hilltop, I could see the town of Sahagún. Excitement rises within me. I have reached the border between Palencia and León. This is another milestone today. The city of León is not too far away from Sahagún. It is another fifty-five kilometers.

Walking a little ways, I could see a statue of Saint James. It is made of iron. I walked up to it and leaned over to touch it. Then I could not help myself. I hugged the statue with all my strength. Here I am holding onto this statue with a firm grip. The goodness of this journey is affirming what I am doing.

"I do not want to let you go. Come with me," I said to the statue. Closing my eyes, I did not want to let go.

"Excuse me, could you please let us know when you are done? We would like to take a picture," a hiker said.

"Oh my, I am sorry. I just got carried away," I replied and smiled. Then I quickly removed myself from the statue and started to walk.

As I crossed over another bridge, the Valderaduey River is beneath my feet. Looking over to the side, I clearly see a reflection of myself.

"Continue your journey today," a little voice whispered.

"Yes. I will pick up my feet and walk," I replied. This bridge leads me into Sahagún. "Today is amazing," I shouted.

The town of Sahagún has an archway, San Benito. The arch is welcoming to folks who come into this incredible town. Entering makes me think how many other pilgrims, like me, have come through here. The simplicity is apparent. The brick images of two churches, San Tirso and San Lorenzo date back to the twelfth and thirteenth century. These ancient structures show the age, and at the same time, they reveal beauty. The San Lorenzo Church tower has open arched windows on all four sides. During this period, Sahagún had many hospices for pilgrims as they made their journey through here. Captured by the beauty, I was still able to find my way to Plaza Mayor, the main square of Sahagún, to rest for a while.

Soaking in the sunlight, I drank water and ate a piece of bread. After a while, I got up and slowly strolled out of Sahagún. I can see why many folks if they need to stop and continue later, would end here. This is magnificent. Those I met along the way and have ended their journey here, I know I will not see again. However, they will be forever in my heart. We have shared something special.

At leaving Sahagún, I came to my fourth bridge and crossed the Cea River. I am leaving Sahagún to walk into the wilderness. This time it is a little different. The temperature is cool and comfortable. Walking a distance, I came to a fork on the path. Going to the right takes me to the Via Traiana which is a rocky terrain. The left side keeps me on the French Road through the woodlands. I decided to go left. Walking in the wooded area, I hear birds chirping in the trees.

As I walk, I am thinking about my father and mother. They are in heaven. Tears begin to wail up in my eyes. Stream of tears flowed like a river. "I miss you, Dad and Mom. You are in a good place. Please watch over me," I sobbed. Keeping silence for a while, I heard footsteps. I will hide my face. Wiping my tears, I pulled my hat visor down so one will see me weeping. This walk helps me to reflect on my past. Today is reflecting on my parents whom I miss dearly.

"Buen Camino," a cheerful voice said.

I looked up. It is my friends from this morning. "Buen Camino. I am glad to see you," I replied.

"Are you fine? Is everything going well with you?" the woman asked.

"I am doing fine. Thank you for asking," I answered.

"Could we walk with you? How far are you walking today?" she asked.

"Of course, please join me. I will be walking to El Burgo Ranero," I said. We looked at each other and smiled. "Let us do this," I said joyfully.

We crossed over little streams along the way. Suddenly, my back leg became painful. I hobbled along. The woman walking with me also had pains in her leg as well. We thought there is no rush in hurrying. Taking our time is the best thing to do for now. Walking further, the terrain became a little rocky.

Seeing a sign nearby the roadway reads El Burgo Ranero. This gave us hope. It is noon. Here we are walking into the village. Every day is getting shorter to our final stop to Santiago de Compostela. We found the albergue. This albergue did not have many bunk beds. There were about twenty-eight bunks. The line for the overnight stay started. Soon the albergue will open.

Placing our bags in line, my friends and I walked over to the store to buy something for dinner. Since we are tired, salad would be a perfect meal for tonight. We picked up vegetables, lettuce, fruits, and fresh bread. After shopping, the albergue opened. My friends and I were one of the last to get a bunk for the night. We are delighted to be here.

After showering, I washed my clothes. I found a clothesline around the side of the albergue. The sun feels good. There is little wind. My clothes will dry in no time. I applied the rubbing ointment on my knee and back of my leg. I am hoping this will take care of this throbbing pain.

As I lay in my bunk, I reflected on today's journey. I walked thirty-one kilometers. The weather continues to be superb. Crossing over four bridges and many streams today brings comfort and joy to me. The tears I shed were not tears of sorrow, but joy. As much as I miss my parents, deep down inside they are with me. They are my guardian angels watching over me as I make this journey.

Falling asleep, I could feel the rivers filling up inside me. It gives me strength. I am not alone.

Day 19 ~ Puente de Villarente

Arches

Today is August 9th. It has been two weeks since I started my pilgrimage. This has been quite an experience. I have enjoyed the wonderful people that I have met along the way. This is not over. I am looking forward to the rest of the journey.

Starting early in the morning brought me cheer and delight. Today will be filled with excitement. "What kind of excitement?" I asked myself.

"You do not know. It is too early to tell," a little voice chirped.

I hurried to start the day. I could see three flashlights shining ahead of me. "Wow! I thought I would be first this morning. Keep in mind there is always someone in front and behind," I laughed quietly to myself. Maybe I could catch up and pass them.

"Slow down speedy. You have come this far so do not try to run a race the rest of the way," the little voice inside me said.

"Okay! I will be calm today. Thank you for being my speed monitor and my compass to keep me on track," I chuckled.

A new day is here. The sunrise dispels darkness. Walking alongside trees keeps everything fresh and clean. Closing my eyes, I can smell the wooded area around me. I breathed in the pine scent. This is healthy for my mind, my body, and my spirit. Breathing deeply balances my walk and keeps my feet on the ground.

By mid-morning, I reached the small village of Reliegos. The first thing that caught my eye was the houses in the village. The architectural design of the homes is adobe. These houses display the uniqueness and characteristics of ancient times in a very simple way.

"This is perfect timing! I feel at home," I shouted. While I was taking out fruit to munch on, I pulled out an old fig. "Wow! Where have you been all this time?" I said to the fig. Turning the fig over a couple of times, I finally bit into it. "Yes, this is so good," I declared in delight. I did not know I had one more piece left. "Yummy, this is good. Food is extremely delicious these days," I said gleefully.

Concentrating on the fig, the walk took me to the crossing of the Grande River. Before I knew it, I had walked into the town of Mansilla de las Mulas. At one time, this town had a monastery, several churches, and pilgrim hospices. As I looked around, I could only see a quaint community. I strolled slowly to a pilgrim's monument. The crucifix is on a three-tier concrete square. Pilgrim statues are gathered below the crucifix. I sat down next to one of the statues to rest.

"Yes, this is what it is all about while making this journey. To sit down and relax for a few minutes," I said softly. Taking out my hose from the camelbak, I leisurely sipped my water. Then I closed my eyes. Tears gently streamed down the side of my face. "I love everything about this walk," I said softly.

"Hello, hello. Are you alive or have you become stone like one of these statues," someone said.

I opened one eye then the other. "Goodness! I am drifting into the cosmos today," I replied.

Waking up from the little catnap, I shook myself.

"Hi! It is so nice to see you. Did you just get here? Where are the other two travelers?" I asked.

"Yes, we just arrived. They are in the little eatery having a snack. I came over to see the monument when I saw you sitting here. You look like you were in a faraway place," she said.

"Yes, I feel very much at home right now," I responded. Grabbing my walking stick, I pulled myself up.

Looking over to the side, we could see our other friends waving. We waved back. Walking over to them, we smiled and hugged each other.

"Buen Camino," I said.

"How far are you trekking today?" one of our friends asked.

"I think I will be going as far as Puente de Villarente," I answered.

"Great! We are thinking about spending the night there as well. Let us all walk together," a friend suggested.

"That will be wonderful," I said with delight.

Before long, I began to lag behind. Although I still could see them, it grew to be at a greater distance. As long as we know Puente de Villarente is our destination tonight, this is fine.

As I came to Porma River, I could not believe my eyes. "Good Heavens! I cannot believe what I am seeing," I said in awe.

Before me is a gigantic bridge with about twenty arches. I could not believe the length of the bridge and this many arches. This is something I would have never imagined. Staring at the bridge my mind could only think of light to my feet.

"Yes, light to my feet," I whispered softly.

As I began crossing the bridge, I repeated a wonderful scripture passage, "Your word is a lamp to my feet and a light to my path," Psalm 119:105. Walking gingerly across I repeated the passage. Staring at the water I pictured in my mind how many other pilgrims crossed this bridge.

"Now, I am one of these pilgrims," I thought proudly.

Taking each step gracefully, my feet felt like they were cushioned. Gliding my way over each archway caused my feet to illuminate along the path. "I will savor this moment forever," I said to myself. Reaching over to the other side of the bridge, I looked back. "My footsteps are now on this bridge for all eternity," I whispered as I bowed humbly.

Just before entering into the village of Puente de Villarente the wind began to pick up. Walking on the roadside I turned to cross a ramp going into the village. I could see three hikers making their way down the ramp. They were walking sideways holding onto the railings. Then a large truck passed by. At that point, I too held tightly against the railing with all my strength. As the truck passed, the wind pulled me up. Looking over to the side, I saw another hiker also holding onto the railing for dear life. Her hat flew up in the air, over the ramp, and landed on the ground below. The truck passed and relief was in sight.

"Whew, that was close. Walking sideways and holding onto the railings is a first for me," I said with relief. Reaching the bottom, I looked around for the other walkers. In the distance, I could see them waving to me.

"Over here, over here Linda," one of them said.

I gather myself together and when I was calm enough to continue, I walked over to them. "Wow, what was that?" I asked.

"The walk going down the ramp was fine. When the wind picked up it became challenging," another hiker said.

"All I could do was hold onto the railings for my life. I felt I was sucked into the wind," I said, once again trembling. "What is important is that we made it. Now, where is the albergue?" I asked after catching my breath.

Dusting off debris from the unnerving and danger-ous episode, we were reassured to see the albergue so close by. Walking into the albergue would not be a problem. There is room for a few more hikers.

"Perfect! In this little albergue, I have a tiny bunk next to a window. This is prime real estate," I said jokingly.

I had to wait my turn for the showers, others who came before me got in first. As I waited, I decided to walk outside and look around. The albergue is U-shaped. It has a high cinder block wall for privacy. There is a little courtyard with green grass.

"Ah, a little bonsai tree," I smiled in admiration. It has a short tree trunk with three thick branches. I walked slowly over to it to see if it is real. "Yes, this is a tree," I said. Sitting under the tree, I closed my eyes and fell asleep.

After a while, I heard noise and laughter. I awakened to see travelers gathering in the courtyard to chat and share a meal. Getting up, I walked to my bunk and headed over to the showers. As I watched the water rinse over me, I could see the dirt running down my tired body. I have not paid much attention to the daily grime that covered my body until now.

"This is amazing what I see and do not see. After all, no two days are alike," I marveled.

Feeling refreshed, I stepped outside of the albergue. In the middle of the town is a church. The church tower looks ancient. The earth-toned tower is well maintained. There are two arched windows on all sides of the tower. Two bird nests sit on the corners atop the tower. A tiny church bell rests inside a steeple. The steeple points high above everything else around it. I can see storks flying around the tower rooftop. As I watched them, I noticed the storks feeding their little ones with their long beaks. I can see little bobbing heads of the tiny storks peaking out of the nests. Their chirping sounds could mean they are hungry. The larger storks fly down to feed the little ones.

"This is cool. These storks have a nest and a place to call home. As for me, I do not have a place to call home at the moment," I said surprising myself. Every day I keep walking and eventually need to find a place to stay each evening. In the back of my mind, I am hopeful there will be a bed, a cot, or a bunk for me tonight.

So far, I have been able to find a place every night. "Is this pure luck or fate?" I asked myself. "I think it is a little bit of both. I am lucky to be here, and fate keeps me going."

As I walked around the four corners of the church, my eyes fixed upon the steeple. I am happy to be here to see the storks feeding their young ones. The view from up there is spectacular. "They have a bird's eye view," I said, humored. Sometimes being high above everything is good, especially for storks.

"I am getting hungry. I need to find a market," I said. I could see the hikers I was with earlier today. I waved to them. "Hi, over here," I said cheerfully.

One of them turned and waved back. "Come here. The market has delicious fruits and vegetables," a friend replied.

"I am coming. Wait for me," I answered.

As I reached the market, my stomach growled. "I am having hunger pangs," I said holding my tummy.

"Get your food. We will wait for you outside," a friend said.

I picked up bananas, apples, oranges, figs, and bread. "I am so happy," I shouted aloud.

"Why are you happy?" a friend asked.

"They have fresh figs. These are favorites for me. I love them," I replied joyfully.

"Come on. Let us go and sit in the courtyard and break bread together," a friend said in excitement.

"Yes, this will be lovely," another friend remarked.

We made our way back to the albergue. As we walked to the courtyard, everyone there clapped with joy. "Yeah, they are finally going to eat," someone shouted.

We all smiled with delight. We blessed our meal, asking to give us strength and nourishment. This is the best time of the day when we share our food and ourselves. We all come together in fellowship. By now, we have seen one another, slept next to each other, walked with one another, and shared our stories and experiences. We are all friends. We all share a common goal. Our goal is Santiago de Compostela. For now, we break bread, eat a meal, and enjoy the beautiful view of a little "bonsai" tree.

When everyone was full and silent, the sound of a flute filled the air. The ambiance is enchanting. We look at one another and smile knowingly our hearts are filled with joy. Then one by one we get up and walk to our bunks. No sound. No noise. Simply silence. Total quiet. We sleep off another day's journey and ready ourselves for tomorrow.

Day 20 ~ León

Radiance

Yippee! I am on my way to León today. This is exciting. It is another milestone. After climbing four small hills, León is then just a stone's throw away. The distance from Puente de Villarente to León is twelve kilometers. It is the shortest walk day. After this, it will be approximately 300 kilometers to Santiago de Compostela. I have already walked 500 kilometers. "I am looking forward to this journey today. It is as if I am on cloud nine," I rejoiced.

I left Puente de Villarente just before dawn. Today, I want to see it change from dark to light instantly. Although the weather conditions are a little chilly, the air feels good to me. I started the hike walking with two of my friends. After a while, we spaced ourselves. Then I withdrew from the group to gather my thoughts for the day.

"Dawn is here," I said aloud.

"Yes, it is," a soft voice replied.

Up ahead, I could see a friend waving his walking stick in the air. This is a wondrous moment. Radiance is everywhere. I am thankful for coming this far. Being humble helps me to be focused. As I think of my accomplishment in reaching León, tears of joy stream down my face. I am blessed and filled with grace.

Passing by the Porma Canal, I see a small hill. Reaching the hilltop, I can see the village of Arcahueja not far away. Walking into the village, I pass a church. There is no one outside on the road.

"This little village is so quiet I can hear my heart beat," I observed. Step by step my footsteps are in tune with my breathing. "Perfect! Walking all these days, this is the first time my heart, breathing, and footsteps are all in sync," I said in delight.

Before long, a sign appears. It reads Valdelafuente. The trail leads to a path over a little bridge. This is another tiny village. There is not much to see, just a few buildings. The quietness is surreal. I am able to walk in cadence. The weather is simply beautiful today.

As I leave Valdelafuente, I can see Alto del Portillo. Up ahead is another hill to climb. These hills are not difficult to hike. The terrain is on a little incline. Sipping my water, I pulled out a fruit to chomp on. Reaching the summit, I am at Alto del Portillo. I can see a tower that overlooks two rivers. In León, I am looking forward to going to San Marcos Square. A fifteenth-century stone cross that was taken from this very summit stands in the square. This will be something special to see.

Leaving the summit, I descended into the last village of Puente del Castro. Crossing over an old bridge, I made my way into the village. The bridge crosses over the banks of the Torio River. As I rested on the bridge, I looked over the side. I could see a reflection of myself.

"From here, I am on my way to León. Although I may not look my best, I feel good inside," I thought aloud. It has been a while since I have seen a big city. Taking a deep breath, I began to hike.

Going across the highway, cars stop to allow walkers to cross over. Back in the day when roads were not developed this was not a concern for hikers. When roads became thoroughfares for transportation, some of the paths were turned into highways. As I am getting over to the other side, I can see a yellow shell marker pointing down toward a narrow path. I stopped for a moment to gaze upon this magnificent view of León. I would have never imagined León to be this large. The weather is so clear I can see the cathedral of León. It stands above all of the other buildings. There is beauty all around.

As morning is disappearing, sunshine elegantly unfolds over the city. It is still cool as I walk down a shrub-gladdened trail. Little factories in an industrial area lead me into León. By mid-morning, I arrive into the city. After making a few turns, I am standing on the cathedral square.

"I cannot believe I am here. This cathedral is bigger than I imagined," I said to myself.

As I looked from the base all the way to the top of the steeples of the cathedral, I could see that the architectural design is magnificent. Amazingly, this cathedral was built around the thirteenth and fourteenth century. Ancient spirals rose up pointing high above all else, as if reaching for the heavens. There is blue sky with no clouds anywhere in sight. Sunlight illuminates the cathedral. The three ancient naves welcome visitors through the doorways. A circular medieval stained-glass window boasts stunning artwork above the nave accents within the splendor of the façade.

"I am looking forward to going into the cathedral. Later will probably be better," I thought. I could not keep still. Moving from one bench to another, I want to see the cathedral from every angle. As I sat, I closed my eyes to absorb and ingrain the extraordinary craftsmanship and antiquities I am experiencing. Sitting here and soaking in the sun, I revel in the fact that this is a free day. I decide I will tour the city.

As I looked around the square, I could see a friend by a café. I waved to him. He waved back. Walking over to him, I noticed he is sitting alone.

"Hello. I am glad to see you. How are you?" I asked.

"It is good to see you, too," he replied.

I looked at him again. "Are you okay?" I asked. Then I could see tears flowing from his eyes. I could see something is troubling him. He looked up at me. "Where is your fiancé? Is she with you?"

"No. She stopped the walk," he sobbed.

"I am sorry to hear this," I said with concern.

"She could not continue the walk. Yesterday, the bottom of her heel tore," he explained.

"I am sorry to hear this. Oh my, this journey is important for you and her. I remembered a few days ago you mentioned this walk is a test for your love for each other," I said with sorrow.

"Yes. Now I am alone," he said bursting into tears. I sat with him and held his hand in comfort. After a while he stopped crying.

"I hope you will continue the walk. If you do not, I will understand. I will keep you and your fiancé in my prayers," I said.

"There is no need for me to continue walking," he said.

"Before you decide, think about it. Maybe your fiancé will want you to continue. Then next year bring her back to where she stopped and walk with her the rest of the way. This would be an expression and experience of true love for both," I suggested.

"Thank you for your kindness. I will think about it," he replied.

Two of our friends showed up. We sat and had hot chocolate. Sitting with a perfect view of the cathedral, we remained silent. After a while, I got up.

"I am going to find a place for the night," I said.

My friends stood up as well. We walked a little way to find an albergue. Checking in the albergue allowed me time to freshen up and then go on an adventure in the city.

I went back to the cathedral. From the outside, I thought it would be dark inside. As I walked in, I was surprised. Sunlight radiates throughout. The stained-glass windows are striking to see. During the day, we can see different lighting on the windows. Next, I am on my way to find San Isidoro Church.

After finding the church, I sat in the chapel. As I sat in silence, my eyes got heavy. I could not keep my eyes open. Before I knew it, I feel asleep. Then I heard a banging sound. I awoke from my nap. "I must be tired," I said to myself.

Looking around, there were a few others in the chapel. After sitting for a little while longer, I got up and walked outside. The sun feels good. I feel wonderful. Walking to the back of the church, I came to the Pantheon of the Kings of León. The remains of twenty-three León monarchs are buried here. This church also has a museum and a library. The frescos go back to the twelfth century. I could spend an entire day here.

Later in the evening, my friends and I walked to a church. There will be a blessing service for the pilgrims. As we walked into the church, we sat toward the front. Several nuns came outside to sit near the sanctuary. They sat in wooden chairs across from each other. The nuns began praying and singing. We joined in. This is a beautiful and introspective evening.

After the service, we went to get a bite to eat. Sitting in the restaurant, we wanted to eat paella. "I have not had paella since the first day at Saint-Jean-Pied-de-Port. That seems like it has been forever," I said aloud.

"Yes, I think we can all agree with you on this," a friend said. We all laughed.

"Everything seems so long ago," another friend replied.

"This is why now that we are in León we need to celebrate a little," I said invitingly.

Then we toasted with our drinks and chatted a little more. When our paella dishes came to the table, we were silent for a little while. Picking up our silverware, in unison we scooped the paella, put it in our mouths as we savored every bit of it. We acted as one. It was a sweet moment of unity. Once we got to the second scoop, however, we were on our own. We shared our stories and enjoyed one another's company.

After dinner, we walked passed the cathedral. The lights illuminated the structure. It is picturesque at night. We sat on the benches and enjoyed the ambiance.

"I would not mind sleeping out here tonight if I did not already have a place to stay," I said.

"I agree with you," a friend replied.

"When I feel like this, I know by now it is time for me to head back to the albergue," I joked.

We stood up and stretched and made our way back to our place. Along the way we stopped for ice cream. It hit the spot.

When we reached the albergue we hugged each other. "Buen Camino to everyone," I said.

We all repeated the same words.

Then I went to see the caretaker for an ice pack. She could only give me a frozen package of vegetables. I took it and went to my bunk. Putting the pack on my knee, I felt a little better. It numbed some of the achiness. A little while later, I returned the package.

In the dark, I found my way back to my bunk and crawled into my sleeping bag. Everyone is still and quiet. I began to take deep breaths. Finding my center point, I could feel my heart beating.

"I am a lucky person. Yes, I do have some aches and pains, but it comes with the walk," I whispered to myself in a soft voice. The walk today is simple and filled with grace.

I remembered my friend and his fiancé. I hope he does not give up walking the rest of the way to Santiago de Compostela. It is for him to decide. I hope his fiancé will come back and pick up from where she stopped. Of course, I will never know this. I will throw it into the cosmos.

Having a free day like today helps it all feel worthwhile. I am looking forward for tomorrow. At this moment, I am at a loss for words to describe how I feel. I think silence is best for now. Turning over onto my side I am settled in to rest for the night. Tomorrow is another adventure on this journey. On the way out of León, I will get to see the stone cross.

Repeating Psalm 46:10, "Be still, and know that I am God," I began drifting to sleep. I continue saying it over again, shortening it each time. Until in the end, "BE."

Day 21 ~ San Martin del Camino

Love

Dawn is upon the city of León. The different shades of yellow, orange, and pink reflect off of the streetlights make for an easy thoroughfare. Leaving the city begins my search for the stone cross at San Marcos Square. Although I feel rested, I still have some pain in my knee. If all goes well, my goal today is to walk twenty-five kilometers to San Martin del Camino.

I inhale the freshness of the morning. My mind is awaken by birds chirping as I make my way through the streets. At one point, I smell fresh bread. The smell goes into my nose. I try very hard to hold it inside. Slowly breathing in and out fills me with energy. I begin to reach into my pocket and take out a piece of bread. I can only imagine this piece of bread is the synergy I am experiencing with this smell. Then a mist and some slight rain clean the air.

"I have a blessing for this morning," I said quietly. Walking in silence clears my thoughts for a little while.

"What is in store for me today? Will the weather be kind? Who will I run into?" I said in my thoughts.

Walking along Renueva Street and Suero de Quiñones Avenue, I finally reach San Marcos. I am standing on the square. Then over my shoulder I see a fifteenth-century stone cross. Below the cross, a statue of a pilgrim is sitting on one of the steps. The statue faces one of León's pilgrim hospitals. It was founded in the eleventh century. Today it is transformed into a luxury hotel; Parador de San Marcos. The façade is spectacular with lights. The exterior captures artworks of long ago.

I make my way over to the cross and sit next to the statue. I gaze at the figure with delight.

"I am sitting next to a pilgrim," I said gleefully. Resting my hand on the statue, I closed my eyes to capture the moment calmly.

"Good Morning! Hello, are you walking today?" a voice said.

I open one eye, then the other. Standing in front of me are friends. "Hello! Good Morning. Yes, I am walking today," I replied.

Before standing up, I lean over to the statue and kiss the cheek of the stone pilgrim. "Thank you for spending time with me," I whispered. Getting to my feet, I wobble a bit. One of my friends bends over and steadies me.

"Thank you for catching me," I said a little embarrassed.

"Not a problem. Where are you going today?" a friend asked.

"I am walking as far as San Martin del Camino," I answered.

"Great! We are going there as well," another friend replied.

We came to a bridge and crossed the Bernesga River. This bridge has several arches. Looking back at the city of León, I feel a little sadden. I am leaving behind a beautiful place filled with culture, art, and hospitality. The trail leads into the town of Trobajo del Camino, which sits on a hill. This town is a part of León. I continue following the path under a roadway and walking along El Camino de la Cruz. I feel a little cold. Clouds began to cover the area.

"I think it is going to rain," I said.

"Yes, it is getting cloudy. I am beginning to feel rain drops. Time to take out our ponchos," a friend replied.

I reached under my rucksack and pulled out my poncho. Just as I finished pulling it over my head, the rain came down hard. "The timing could not have been better," I said to myself.

Continuing on, we walked under another roadway. The village of La Virgen del Camino, or in English, the Virgin of the Road, is not far away. There is a story about this village. In the 1500's, the Virgin appeared to a villager. The Virgin asked the man to have a chapel built there. To convince the bishop he saw the Virgin, the man put a rock in his sling. As the rock was slung, it turned into a boulder. A sanctuary was built and dedicated to the Virgin. Today, this is one of the favorite sites to visit. The architectural design looks quite modern. The Virgin is in the center of the façade above the entryway. Standing on either side of the Virgin are Apostles resting on the ledge, welcoming pilgrims. The Apostle, Saint James, points with his right hand toward the Camino.

Approaching a fork in the road, I have two choices. I will need to decide which way to go. I could stay on the path, or walk inland. Both paths will merge at Hospital de Órbigo. Since I am stopping overnight at San Martin del Camino, the trail I am on will take me there. My friends also decided to do the same.

The rain stopped. By now, my tummy is rumbling. "It is time for me to have a snack," I said cheerfully. Taking out a fig, I began to chew it. "This is fresh. Is anyone hungry for a fig?" I asked.

"I think I am ready for one," a friend replied.

"Here you go, enjoy it!" I answered.

"Wow, this is good," my friend said.

Drinking water to wash down the tiny seeds helped to fill my tummy.

Love

After a while, we reach the village of Valverde de la Virgen. As we walk down the road, a friend spots a bench with baskets. We walk over to the bench. A gentleman comes out of his house. He looks at us and he smiles.

"Buen Camino," he said. Then he points to the fruits and nuts. He signals us with his hand to take some for our journey. Behind the baskets, we see a sign. I could not make out what the sign says, but I did recognize the word *peregrino,* which means pilgrim. This we are. In one of the baskets, there is a Spanish flag. As we look in the baskets, we help ourselves to the treats.

"Thank you for your kindness and generosity," I said with gratitude. My friend also thanks the gentleman.

"This is simply amazing. The generosity offered us today is a basket of fruits and nuts for hikers," I said in appreciation.

"People do care for us," a friend added.

"This will fill me for the rest of the day," I remarked.

"Me, too," a friend chuckled.

"These folks have grateful hearts," I said with delight. We walked and ate the fruits and nuts along our way. They are tasty and juicy.

Since the rain has stopped, I took off my poncho. Rolling it up, I slipped it back into my rucksack. Then I waved to my friends, saying, "Buen Camino."

Feeling content, I began to walk alone until I came to the village of San Miguel del Camino. The Páramo plains begin from this area. I can see cornfields far into the distance. The cornfields blanket this region. With a little breeze blowing, the tips of the cornfields waved lightly in the wind. This is a beautiful sight to see.

Although the weather is a little uncomfortable, it is still tolerable. Trekking along the way, I see two hikers. "Oh, my goodness I do not believe this," I said with excitement.

Moving along quickly, I catch up with them. I had met these two brothers at the beginning of my walk. The older brother, heavier in weight, had a walking problem. A year ago, the younger brother walked the Camino. He invited his older brother to do the hike with him. Because of his circumstances, his younger brother would assist him walking. While the brother assisted him along the way, the larger fellow moved very slowly during the walk.

"Buen Camino," I said.

They turned and smiled. "Hello. How are you?" one of them asked.

"I am doing fine. This is a delight to see you both," I answered. "You look so good. Where is all the weight you started with a few weeks ago?" I asked in amazement.

"Thank you. I left all the weight back there," he said laughing aloud. He turned around and pointed in the direction of the roadway. His younger brother could not help but chuckle. We walked together for a while.

"How far are you walking today?" one of the brothers asked.

"I am going as far as San Martin del Camino," I replied. "How far will you travel today?" I asked.

"We are going as far as Hospital de Órbigo. Then it all depends on the weather," the other brother answered.

After walking a while, I pick up my speed and headed on down the trail. "Buen Camino. Take care. I hope to see you again," I said. Then I waved good-bye for now.

"Yes, we hope to see you again. Take care of yourself. Buen Camino," one of the brothers replied.

As I walked, I could not help but think of these brothers. One of them did this walk last year. This year, two brothers are doing the journey together. This is love. Brothers caring for each other are wonderful to see.

After a short distance, I could see a sign saying Villadangos del Páramo. "I need to take a break," I said softly.

As I entered into the village I saw a church. Walking into the church, I open the door and find a spot to sit for a little while. Then I see a statue of Saint James. He has a three-cornered hat with crosses and shells. This sculpture looks interesting. The shells caught my eye.

Looking at them, I reached for my shell on my rucksack. I held it tightly. I felt moved by it.

"Thank you, Lord for bringing me here today," I said quietly. As I stayed in stillness, I could feel a chill in my body. This made me feel good inside. Walking out the church, I feel at peace.

I need to continue walking if I want to make it to San Martin del Camino today. Soon, the area became cool. Crossing over a stream, I began to walk in a wooded area. Although I was trekking in the woods, I could hear traffic. The pathway is alongside a highway. After walking another five kilometers, I will arrive at San Martin del Camino. Before long, I could hear footsteps behind me.

"Hello. We are glad we caught up with you," a voice called out.

I turned my head. "Oh my, I am glad to see you," I said gleefully. They are the same friends I walked with earlier today.

"Where have you been?" one of them asked me.

"I have been in this town for awhile. I visited a church," I replied.

"It is meant to be," another friend said.

"Why?" I asked.

"Let us find an albergue at San Martin del Camino. We can share our stories from today," a friend added.

"This will be wonderful," I responded in awe.

Love

In no time we reach the village of San Martin del Camino. For the night, our stay is at a charming albergue. Over dinner, I shared the exciting thing that I experienced today. I told them about meeting up with the two brothers. I could not get over how well the struggling brother is doing. In the beginning, we all thought he would not make it this far. Every ten to twenty steps he would stop to catch his breath. Now, he has passed us. He and his brother are on their way to the next town. Fantastic!

We laughed about our episodes of the day. Tomorrow will here before we know it. Gradually our conversation came to an end for the evening. We wish each other a "Buen Camino." Hugging one another we walk to our sacks.

Looking at my rucksack, I decide to get rid of one more plastic bag. The bag contains a T-shirt, a first aid kit, and bandages. It will reduce the baggage I am carrying. This plastic bag will be good for someone else. I gave the bag to the albergue caretaker. They are happy to receive items because someone new comes along has needs.

Reflecting back over today, I recall the three thoughts from this morning. Hiking today fills me with happiness and joy. Having little expectation in life sometimes can be the happiest moments to encounter. Today, I experienced love for others.

Day 22 ~ Astorga

Majestic

*B*oom, *Boom, Crash!* I awoke to sounds.
"What is this noise?" I asked myself. I waited to hear the sounds again. It is a storm. I got up and walked over to the window. As I pulled the curtains back, I could see the rain. Water is everywhere. The wind is blowing madly in all directions. I could hear the thunder and see the lightning.

"Oh my, I hope this is not another August 6th," I said with a gulp. Moving slowly, I picked up my rucksack and squeezed it tightly. Looking at my watch, I saw that I will be getting up in about two hours to start my journey for the day.

As I sit in deep thought, I realize the days are going by quickly. I feel confident walking every day. My clothing is sagging, which means I am losing weight. My rucksack and I are one now. I begin to grip it firmly to my chest as I hear more wind, rain, thunder, and lightning. My rucksack has become a part of me.

Getting rid some of my things from inside of my rucksack has helped. Although many times I considered giving up my rucksack, I could not and would not give it up. I do not feel the weight of it on my shoulders anymore. I love my rucksack. I love my walking stick and hat. I love my shoes, and my jacket, and little bread and fruits I carry each day. These are my essentials that has brought me this far.

After a while the pounding weather subsided. I cannot go back to sleep now. It is time to get ready and hike another day. Making my way to the bathroom, I took my time. This morning I am not in any particular hurry. Walking in clear weather is better than trampling through muddy trails and slippery slides.

Opening the front door of the albergue, I could see clouds. These clouds did not look black and heavy. In fact, they look pretty good. I could see on the horizon that dawn is upon us once more. A silver lining breaks through darkness.

As I head out the door, I look ahead down the muddy trail. This will not be difficult to trek as long as I stay on path. The morning freshness pecks at my cheeks. Suddenly, I sneeze.

"The air is extra fresh this morning. This is a wonderful way to wake up," I whispered softly. Taking in deep breaths, I slowly make my way out of San Martin del Camino. If it does not rain, I will walk twenty-three kilometers to the city of Astorga. This will be another interesting city to see. I am thrilled because there is a cathedral there. Next to it is the Bishop's Palace. If all goes well, Astorga will be my overnight stay.

The morning sunlight is on the mountains. Rainbow colors glow on the mountaintops. The sky slowly lights up with red, dark orange and yellow ribbons in the shape of a bow. I give glory and thanksgiving to God. In praise, I reflect on Psalm 62:1-2:

> For God alone my soul waits in silence;
>   from him comes my salvation.
> He alone is my rock and my salvation,
>   my fortress; I shall never be shaken.

I believe I am not alone on this journey. God is my shield and protector. If I am strong, it is because God gives me the strength to do what I need to do every day. Deep down inside, I feel the awesomeness of what I am doing is exactly the right thing for me to do. Throughout this journey, I am not alone. Something greater and more powerful than I is with me.

As the earth is lighted, I am surrounded by fields of wheat. The smell simply excites my sense of smell. In a distance, I can see water. The Órbigo River is nearby.

Entering into Puente de Órbigo, the two walk-ing paths are joined into one. Quick to my feet, I am standing halfway on a magnificent bridge, the Paso Honroso, which means the Honorable Passage. There is an amazing story about this bridge. Back in the fourteenth century, events took place here. A knight would fight in a tournament for the love of a maiden and for his freedom. The tournament would last for several days. After winning the tournament, the knight would take his prize and make his way to Santiago de Compostela as a pilgrim. This journey never ceases to amaze me. The history, culture, and traditions continue to unfold along the way.

Crossing a medieval bridge, I am in Hospital de Órbigo. Close by is a parish church. Making my way to the church, I stopped to rest. Sitting on the steps in the front, I can see a few pilgrims walking. One waves his hat.

"Who could this be?" I asked myself. As they came closer, I realized they stayed at the same albergue as I did.

"Good Morning. How are you today?" a friend said.

"Good Morning. I am doing fine. Thank you," I replied.

"Did you enjoy the weather back at the albergue last night?" another friend asked.

"I woke up to it and shivered to my wits end," I said jokingly.

"How far are you hiking today?" another friend asked.

"I am going to Astorga. How about you-all?" I remarked.

"Astorga as well," they replied.

"Great, I have rested enough. Let us begin our journey," I said.

Reaching the tiny village of Villares de Órbigo, the smell of garlic tickled my nostrils. This village is known for raising garlic. The garlic wafts out from the village. Looking down at the canal, I saw much shrubbery along the path. The plants near the canal banks are healthy and strong. The foliage is colorful.

Upon climbing a hill, I spotted the small community of Santibáñez de Valdeiglesias up ahead. Walking through this community, I came to La Iglesia de la Trinidad. It is a church. Gazing at the façade, the architecture is done in a reddish-brown color stone. Two bells high-above begin to ring throughout the area. It is mid-morning. Heading out of the village, I can see my friends up in the distance. This is fine. We will meet again in Astorga.

Walking up another hill, chestnut trees are along the road. "I love chestnuts. It is sad that I cannot have any for now," I thought. The forest and trees offer a lot of shade along the trail.

As I pass over the next hill, I can see that the Saint Toribio Cross is near. Seeing a few friends standing near the cross, I speed up my steps.

"Hello everyone, I made it," I said with a big smile.

One of my friends turned and answered, "We are happy to see you."

"I am happy to be here. It is amazing to look at this cross," I replied happily.

At the top of the cross, a historical work of art rests. I could not make it out. Astorga is not too far away. Many little stones around the cross indicate countless people have come through here. Each places a stone at the foot of the cross. I have reached another milestone on my journey. I am ready to walk to Astorga and call it a day.

Going down a hill, I leave behind San Justo de la Vega. I begin to cross a bridge over the Tuerto River. With very few footsteps, I enter into the city of Astorga. This city goes back two thousand years—simply incredible. Looking around, I can see a lot of pilgrims.

Now I need to find a place to stay for the night. Checking into the albergue is simple. The bunks are ready for the pilgrims. After I quickly freshen up, I go back out to explore this ancient city.

Walking down one of the streets in the town, I team up with some of my friends. As I came to a drugstore, I could not believe my eyes.

"Oh my goodness!" I said aloud.

"Are you all right?" one of my friends asked.

"Yes, but I need to stop here for a moment," I answered.

"What is it?" another friend asked.

"It is this sign at the drugstore. The sign reads 'Aloha,'" I exclaimed. "This word in the Hawaiian language means hello, greetings, good-bye, love, and many other things. I wonder if the owner is from Hawaii," I said excitedly.

Today is Sunday. The store is closed. I have the urge to climb up to the sign to hug and embrace it. Tears of joy filled my eyes and begin streaming down my face.

"I feel as if I am at a home away from home. Journeying this far, then to see a sign of Aloha this is what it is all about," I shouted with enthusiasm.

One of my friends came over and hugged me. "You are experiencing a blissful moment now," she said.

"Yes, I am. I miss home," I said with sadness. Pulling myself together, the tears stopped.

"Thank you for being here for me," I said to my friend.

"You are welcome. Are you fine to walk around the town?" she asked with concern.

"Yes, I just got caught up in the moment. I will be fine. I am hungry. Let us have lunch," I suggested.

My friends and I walked over to a little café. We ordered sandwiches and ate in the town square. While we were eating, more hikers walked into the town. The sun feels good. This turned out to be a beautiful day. My spirits are lifted again.

After lunch, we walked to the Bishop's Palace. "Wow, this is beautiful," a friend said.

"Yes, it sure is," I replied.

The architectural design shows the decorative windows within the structure. This palace was completed in the early nineteenth century. The entryway into the palace hosts beautiful archways. Although this is not a large structure, it still stands tall. The simplicity is splendid. The weather is stunning with blue skies and cotton ball clouds.

Looking over my shoulder the cathedral is in perfect view. The cathedral was completed in the fourteenth century. A low retaining wall separates the palace from the cathedral. The artistic detail is exquisite. The bronze double-doors of the cathedral exhibit beauty and strength. One that leads into the cathedral tells the Biblical story of the Old Testament in a semi-rotunda. Sculptures protruding from the walls are carved in intricate detail. Taking all this in, I make my way inside to visit the museum, the archives, and the sacristy. Worship, culture, and service exemplify this cathedral. Stepping outside of the cathedral, I gaze upon the magnificence and beauty.

"Hello. What are you doing for dinner?" someone asked.

Looking over my side, I could see a couple. "Hello. I am not doing anything special for dinner," I replied. "I would be delighted to join you for dinner."

"What are we waiting for? A restaurant here we come," the couple suggested.

Walking with my friends, we see other friends along the way. Then we get in line behind the couple. Finally reaching a restaurant for pilgrims, we see other friends as well.

"This is great! We are not alone," I said laughing. Finding a table is not a problem. We sit and share our stories over pasta and salad.

By evening, we make our way back to the albergue. Before we get back, our group passes by the cathedral and the palace. The apse and façade is illuminated. Splendid! The Bishop's Palace stands to the side beautifully lit.

"This is majestic," I said pinching myself.

Darkness is upon us. Beautiful colors of blue, purple, a little pink fill the sky. The cathedral and palace light up the earth reaching toward the heavens.

Day 23 ~ Rabanal del Camino

Simplicity

Beginning at five o'clock in the morning, I make my way down the street passing the cathedral. Stopping to look at the cathedral before I start my walk gave me inspiration. Taking three deep breaths, I turn and head on down the street. I am on my way out of the city. Walking from Astorga to Rabanal del Camino is about twenty kilometers.

Surprisingly, I could feel little raindrops. I look up but could not see the rain because of the cloud cover and it is still dark. I choose to take my chances and continue through the rain for now. No waiting around. I have got to get a move on. Today's journey will require hiking uphill an extra 300 meters in altitude.

Passing through several streets, crossing a bridge, and under a bridge, I head in the direction of Murias de Rechivaldo. After walking a few kilometers the sunrise bring the morning light.

"Great! This is not good," I said. The clouds look dark and it is overcast. "I hope it clears," I whispered and folded my hands in a brief moment of prayer. Walking under another bridge, I know I am on the right path.

Walking through a wooded area, I see yet another bridge. After crossing the Jerga River, I reach Murias de Rechivaldo. This area is known as the Maragato region. It is a small community with old culture still alive with its customs. Many of the houses in this area are made of stone. Walking through the narrow roadway, I pass by some of the old stone houses. Interestingly, there are stone crosses that lead me out the village. No one is outside at this early hour.

As I walk through the hills and more wooded areas, sheep and cows are my entertainment. Cows are in the pasture grazing on the grass along a hillside. Sheepherders walk with their flock. It is a pleasant sight to see. As the herd passes, their smell fills my senses. I move to the side of a narrow roadway to let the sheep pass. Dust fills the air. Slowly the sheep make their way. Some walk right up to me and brush up against my side. They sniff at my rucksack with great curiosity. Their wool is thick. I recognize a few pregnant female sheep. This is special for me to see.

I am still. The best thing I can do is to stay calm and to let the sheep sniff at me. I am not moving. "I am a statue on the journey," I chuckled. In the meantime, my heart is beating faster than fast. Then a deeper calmness comes over me.

"Stay put and keep still," a little voice whispers.

Looking at the sheep, I smile. Seeing their drooping eyes looking up at me, I realize they are perhaps just as excited as I am. After all, I look and smell different.

"I am sorry if I am in your way. Please do not trample me," I said with utmost respect. Then I begin to hum softly, "The sheep have the right-of-way." Politely, again I smile at them.

As the last sheep passes by, I look toward the sheepherder leading them. He turns to look back at his flock. Everything is fine. Dust is now settling. I can continue my walk to the next village.

"This is fun," I said beaming. Taking a washcloth out from my jacket, I wet it and wipe my face. Dirt is all over the cloth. This will be fine. The sheep have left and I need to brighten myself up.

After leaving Murias de Rechivaldo, I begin a gradual climb. The trees bring shade. Upon reaching the tiny village of Santa Catalina de Somoza, it is still somewhat overcast. For now, a little cloud cover helps to give me the energy to continue trekking along.

Passing by a church, I stop to rest for a few minutes. I hear birds chirping above the façade. Reaching into my jacket, I take out a fig, biting into it.

"Could these birds be singing especially for the hikers as we pass through the village?" I said curiously. Listening to the birds a little while longer, I decide I have rested enough. Picking myself up, I begin to hike once again.

As I continue climbing to higher ground, I can feel a little ache in my knee. "After a few days, my aches are back. I guess no pain, no gain," I mumbled to myself. However, I need to keep my balance and stay on course, if I want to reach Rabanal del Camino today.

Some of the wooded area and shade have now disappeared. The next village is not too far away. Then to my surprise, I hear chattering. As I turn, I can see a few friends. I stop and wait for them to catch up.

"Hello, hello," I said aloud.

"Hello to you as well," a friend yelled back. As they get nearer, I join in the group. We laughed about the sheep. One of the sheep pecked at a friend's rucksack, but there was no harm done.

"The sheep are fun," I commented.

"Yes, indeed they are. We are strangers to them," another friend replied.

El Ganso is nearby. This small village has some of the best Maragato architecture. Some of the houses have thatched roofs, which are unique to this village. Walking here is charming. I do not see anyone around. The narrow road takes me into this old village that once had a hospital and a monastery. Apparently, neither remains today.

Hiking upward, I can see my destination for today. Walking into the village of Rabanal del Camino at half-past eleven in the morning is delightful. My friends and I do not see others.

"Are we the first ones here?" I asked.

"It looks like it," one of my friends replied.

Making our way further into the village, we found our overnight accommodations. "Wonderful! I think we need to set up a line for check-in," I said with joy.

A religious order runs this albergue. It also has a retreat center. If a pilgrim wants to stay three days, they could stay at the retreat center. Staying only one night, the albergue would be the place. Two of my friends were deciding on one or three nights. Sometimes hikers stay at places like this to rest longer. Or perhaps they need to search to find themselves. For me, I will stay one night and hike again tomorrow.

We placed our rucksacks at the front entrance of the albergue. Signs posted on the front door indicate they will open at two o'clock in the afternoon. The stone structure looks old and yet in some ways quite modern. Shutters are open to let the fresh air in. They could be cleaning for the next group.

The church bells ring. Following the sound, I walk to the other side of the road. I enter into the church.

BLISS

Mass will start soon. I sit and wait patiently. Everything is quiet and still. A few others come in.

After Mass, I could not believe my eyes. "Look at all of these rucksacks. There are at least fifty rucksacks lined up going down the road," I said amazed. There is a wide assortment of colors, shapes, and sizes of rucksacks.

"Yes, it is the time of day for the next group to be arriving," a friend commented.

As I looked around, I gazed at the albergue. Above the windows, I could see a stone statue of Saint James. Here he stands humbly with a walking stick, carrying a gourd, and a shell.

"This is cool," I said softly. I sense a peaceful aura here. The simple beauty brings out the radiance of this place. I thought maybe one day if I come back here I would stay longer.

Since we have time to spare, my friends and I walked around the town to find a market. Finding it, we bought fruits, vegetables, and bread for our meal tonight. Walking back to the albergue, the doors are open for check-in. After getting stamped, the care-taker reminded me my credential book is full. I will need to pick up a new credential book at my next stay tomorrow.

After all this time, it is so nice to be one of the first to check-in at an albergue. It seems a privilege to be first in line. We get to choose our bunks. I look around carefully, choosing which bunk I will sleep on tonight. Since I am leaving early in the morning tomorrow, I choose a bunk near the front door.

Peering into my rucksack, I bring out the things I use for my daily freshening up. In the showers, I let the water wash all the dirt away. Touching on my knee, I can feel some pain. I will need to ice it and relax. This means no walking around the village. It is my good fortune that the church is just across the way.

After having a bite to eat, a few friends and I make our way over to the chapel for a prayer service. Before the service starts, I walk over to see a construction area inside the chapel. The ground is partially excavated. This reminds me so much of the forum in Rome. Once the service began, we gathered on the other side of the chapel. After the service, I lit a candle for my family back home. I prayed for them, hoping they are in good health. I also prayed for all of the hikers to keep well and have Buen Camino.

Stepping outside the chapel, I gingerly walk down the roadway. I will not walk too far because of my knee. This interesting little village has a unique pathway leading in and out. It is narrow. Cobblestone lines this path. Everything is stone here; roads, buildings, houses, chapel and even the albergue are made of stone. Everything is made from the elements of the earth.

BLISS

Before retiring for the evening, once again, I walked over to the chapel and I am prayed over. This is such a good feeling knowing I am blessed to continue my journey. I feel I am strengthened in spirit after I am blessed. My friends receive blessings as well. We do not know tomorrow might bring, but getting up in the morning will begin new adventures. Most likely there will be more mountains, hills, valleys, bridges, villages, and animals along the way, and challenges to look forward to.

After our blessing, we stayed in the chapel a little while longer. We wished each other a good night's rest. After hugging, one by one walked across the way to our albergue to retire for the night.

Stepping outside of the chapel, I see beauty in the night. It is dark. I am happy it did not rain. Looking up, the stars are bright tonight. A sweet chill runs through my body. I feel nourished and strengthened. This helps me feel worthy in what I am trying to do.

"I am glad to be here," I said quietly.

Making my way over to the caretaker, I picked up an ice pack for my knee. Finding my bunk, I snuggle into my sleeping bag and apply the ice pack. Reflecting back on this day back to Murias de Rechivaldo where the sheep sniffed at me. I truly was in their neighborhood. Thank goodness I did not overreact and had the presence of mind to stay still. This is my highlight for today.

Simplicity is here. Life is simple. On this journey, I am learning a little more about myself and about the Camino. I am realizing that the Camino is offering me the opportunity to love others I meet along the way. I am shedding my old self and filling myself with love. I am discovering a better version of myself. Although this journey is long, I do not regret a single day. By letting go, I am becoming the woman I hope to be.

Day 24 ~ Molinaseca

Wonderment

My alarm just went off. It is five o'clock in the morning, everyone else is still asleep. I tiptoe to the bathroom. I can hear whispering. After a quick washing up, I pick up my hat, shoes, rucksack, and walking stick. I quietly walk out the front door. Sitting on a stone step, I put on my shoes. Breathing in the morning air, I held it in for as long as I could. Then I slowly exhale. I feel sad that I am leaving Rabanal del Camino. I wish I could stay a little longer here. After a few minutes though, my thoughts come back to today's hike.

As I was picking up my stick, I could see the yellow marker. Passing the church, I make my way up a narrow street. I am leaving the area of Astorga. I need to get to Foncebadón before sunrise.

"Today is a special day," I said quietly.

I stretch my hand around my back to feel for the little flat pebbles on the side of my rucksack. Before I left Germany, a very good friend gave me two little flat white rocks.

"Since you are doing this walk, take this with you. One is yours and the other is mine. When you reach Foncebadón, you will know what to do," my friend said.

"Thank you. I will cross that point when I get there," I said in confirmation. Today is here. I am looking forward to getting to Foncebadón.

"This hike is much steeper today than yesterday," I whispered to myself. With my flashlight, I can see a lot of trees in the forests all along the path. I hear something and perk up.

"Good morning. Would you please share your light with me?" a voice said.

I stop and turn to check if this is just my imagination. "This is too early in the morning. Am I hearing things?" I ask myself. Once again, I hear the voice.

"Would you please share your light this morning?" the voice repeated.

I am not hearing things. Someone is in distress. I will do what I can. "I am here. Yes, I will share my light with you. Do you see the light?" I offered. I begin to shine my flashlight in the direction of the hiker.

"Yes, I do," the voice said.

"I will not go any further. I will wait for you," I said louder.

"Thank you. I am getting closer," the voice answered.

"Who could this be? What happen to this hiker's light?" I thought to myself.

In a little while, a woman appears. She is very tall and slender. Wearing a flannel jacket, dark pants, a rucksack and a hat, she looks in distress.

"Good morning. I am happy you are here. My flashlight is out. I have been walking in the darkness until I saw your light. Thank goodness for you," she said nervously.

"I am glad to share my light with you. I do know the feeling. Last week, my flashlight went out in the middle of a storm. Someone helped me as well," I replied.

"Thank you," she said.

"Today it is my turn to help someone in distress," I commented.

Having a flashlight in good working order is extremely important. It offers light to everyone. As we started to walk, a few others join us.

"This morning we have a walking group. We will reach Foncebadón soon," I said.

Everyone is silent. Climbing becomes extreme. The terrain is tough and rocky. At times, I could feel myself slipping. Placing my walking stick in front of me with each step helps me to pull my tired body uphill. I hear clop, clop.

"What is that?" one of the hikers asked.

"I do not know. I hope it is not what I am thinking," I answered.

"What are you thinking?" another hiker asked.

Then I hear the clop, clop again. A blowing sound follows.

"We have visitors. Two large visitors," someone from behind the line said.

"Are they horses?" I asked with concern.

"Yes, we have horses. Two," the same voice said.

I could hear whinnying sounds and low growls. "I think we are in their path. Let us not be frightened," I said.

"I think you are right," the hiker replied.

"Okay, I am moving three steps to my left," I directed.

"We are, too," the others echoed.

The climb is becoming steeper. I am slipping on rocks. I could feel the blowing sounds as the horses snorted nearby. Their huffing noise came closer. I take three more steps to the left. Then the horses seem to scream. I could feel their breath. This is too close for me.

As I turn my head, I could see the horse's dark eyes staring down at me. The horse seems to be commanding me to get out of the way. I stop hiking. They brush up against my shoulder. The two horsemen are looking at me angrily. They are large and look fearsome. The horsemen both wore large hats. They held the reins in one hand. In the other hand, they held their lanterns to light the trail. Light is key. The first horse passes by, then the other. Each makes their way up the steep hill. Of course, we were in their way. This is obvious.

We all stay silent as if we are statues. After they pass, we wait to catch our breath. I let out a big sigh of relief.

"Are we ready to continue our hike," a friend asked.

"Yes, we are ready," each replied.

"Wonderful, let us climb to the summit," someone directed.

"We can do this," another friend encouraged.

Up ahead as daybreak appears, I see a tall shaped object. I am in awe. At this moment, I want to take in everything I am. I stare at the monument.

"We have arrived," a friend said in delight.

This is the Cruz de Ferro, The Cross, a famous monument. An iron cross rests at the top of the tall figure. As the morning breaks through, light shines upon the monument. All around it is dark blue. Gradually, it turns into a softer blue. The quietness seems surreal. At the foot of the monument lay a large pile of rocks. This is an important mark on the trail. Pilgrims place their rocks, one by one, at the foot of this monument.

There are a number of reasons pilgrims place a rock at the monument. One is to signify that I have been here. It is a milestone in the journey. Another reason is that the rock represents our misgivings. Leaving the rock symbolizes our misgivings are behind us.

BLISS

"I am glad to have come this far in the journey. This is my personal reason for leaving my rocks," I said humbly. I reach into my rucksack. Bringing out the two flat white pebbles, I squeeze them tightly. Something comes over me. I could feel a little breeze on my face. I am beginning to see the end of this journey is near.

"Wow, I am in a state of wonderment," I said quietly. As I make my way over to the monument, morning breaks through fully. I walk up to the pile of rocks. I kneel and place the two small rocks at the base of the monument. One rock for me; the other rock is for my friend in Germany.

Touching the monument, I say a prayer. I feel blessed today to come this far. This is a milestone. I rise and I walk down from the pile of rocks to the other side. Today is a breakthrough. Looking around, I could not find anyone I walked with earlier this morning.

"Where are my friends? Where are they? I will catch up with them later," I chuckled.

The sunlight is here. I am walking alone. Silence surrounds me. I can still feel the gentle breeze on my face.

Descending down the summit is a challenging experience. Loose rocks are everywhere. Hiking on crumbling stone is tough. Bells ring. Bicycles are on the path again today. I move to the side. In a flash, they zoom by. A hand waves in the air.

"Buen Camino," bicyclists call out.

"Buen Camino," I reply in greeting.

Before long, I am walking into the small town of Manjarín. I see a few friends.

"Hello," I said.

"How are you?" a friend asked.

"I am fine. After surviving the morning venture, I think I will surely make it the rest of the way today," I said with a smile.

"Where will you stop today?" a friend asked.

"I do not know, but I will walk as far as I can," I replied.

As the trail gets shorter to Santiago de Compostela, finding an albergue is becoming difficult. Other routes coming from Portugal and Spain join in on the same route. The most interesting part of it all will be to see what albergues are still available. I am not worried because I have my sleeping bag. The sky, the moon, and the stars will be fine for me to sleep under.

Making my way out of town, beautiful trees are on both sides of the path. Trekking up a hill, I can feel the pull in my back legs. The good thing is I do not feel pain in my knee. One foot in front of the other keeps me grounded. This is a good sign. Today is a beautiful day for a hike.

After walking a while, I see a sign that reads El Acebo. At the entrance of the village, a stone cross welcomes us. Next to the cross is a water fountain. I refill my camelbak. A narrow road takes me through this village. From here, I begin a gradual descent all the way to the next village. The drop is from 700 meters. I keep imagining this is like sliding down a long flume. The distance will be at least eight kilometers.

"By the time I reach the bottom, I hope to have my feet and legs intact. Here I go," I said with a promising little laugh.

The path is thick with trees. Dry shrubs on both sides of the path make it hot and sticky. The good thing about this part of the walk is that it is goes downhill. I pick up speed. This will be a quick hike. Going downward is not my forte. I find I cannot seem to keep my balance. This is a test for me today.

Suddenly, I have the urge to go to the bathroom. I need to find some bushes to do my humanly nature thing. I find a perfect spot. Slipping into a perfect little hideaway, I smell a sweet fragrance. This is a perfect spot. I do not need any deodorizer. Turning my head, I see a bunch of flowers. Perfect! They are lavender and bright as can be.

"This is a relief. I feel lighter," I laughed looking up to the sky while I do my important business. Then I get up and straighten myself up.

Once again, I put one foot in front of the other and head down the trail. I zoom along down the hill. As I go down into a deep gorge, I find the terrain is again harsh. By now, my knees are feeling the stress of the downhill repetition.

Midway, I come to a little village, Reigo de Ambrós. Chestnut trees surround it. The smells tingle my senses. The stone houses are unique in a different way here. There are decorated balconies hanging over the houses to provide shelter. The stone chimneys are large to accommodate for the severe winters here.

On a slope is the Santa Maria Magdalena Church. This is goes back to the sixteenth century. Its bell towers peek above the village. Houses are built around the church. This is a quaint community. In a distance, I can see the next town, Molinaseca.

Walking through a gorge, I make my way over a bridge. As I cross over the Meruelo River, I enter into Molinaseca. This is the place I will find an albergue. Through the village, I find my overnight stay.

"This looks like a place I need to stay for the night," I said softly. As I make my way into the albergue, a nice gentleman welcomes me. I ask him for an ice pack for my knee. After showering, I lie down and ice my knee. Sleeping is the best activity for me now. I will need energy for tomorrow.

Day 25 ~ Villafranca del Bierzo

Messages

Wide-awake this morning, I am eager to hike. The town of Ponferrada seems interesting. Leaving so early in the morning, I could hear dogs barking along the way.

"I hope there are no loose dogs. I do not want to be in a dog fight this morning," I said calmly. Keeping my eyes and ears open this morning are important. Gripping my hand on my walking stick, I trek through the little road. I said a prayer as I walked.

"Hush! Be quiet," I whispered. Then there is silence. I am at ease. No barking sounds.

As I pass alongside of the Templars' Castle in the town, it gives me strength. The medieval stone castle is lit highlighting the beautiful architectural design. Many columns spiral above the castle walls. The balconies are elegant. From the effects of a little breeze, the castle flags fly proudly in the wind. Leading up to the castle are wide stone gravel walkways. Moats separate the castle from the town. Stone archways connect the town to the castle.

Following markers, I continue on a footpath and go through a tunnel. Walking past green grapevines, I stop to look down at next the village of Columbrianos. This is one of the oldest villages in this area. The crisp air brings in the morning scents of a fresh day. I could not help but to take deep breaths. Green rolling hills and valleys welcome me as I enter into this village. This is the region of Bierzo. The crops in this region are fruits and vegetables. Thoughts of fruits and vegetables stimulate my appetite.

Soon I could hear voices. Aha, hikers are in sight. They are taking a morning break. "Good morning. Buen Camino," I said.

One of hikers turned her head. "Buen Camino to you," she replied with a smile.

"It looks like it is going to rain today," I said.

"Yes, we need to make sure our rain gear is ready for this morning," she answered.

Saying good day to the group, I continue to walk. Trekking up hill, I see farmlands. The rain begins to fall to the ground. I reach for my poncho. I slip it over my head. "A little rain will not hurt me today," I said with enthusiasm.

This area is surrounded by beautiful hills. All of this area is a part of Ponferrada. The greenery is fantastic.

I realize the rain keeps the area abundantly alive and lush. The rain this morning could do some good. In very little time, I arrive in the village of Fuentes Nuevas.

During the next two kilometers, I walk in the tiny village of Camponaraya. Vineyards surround the town. The lush terrain produces hearty wine for the Bierzo region. Taking a break here, I eat a piece of bread, and take a sip of water from my camelbak. As I look to the side, I see a water fountain. I refill my camelbak. The mist and rain have not stopped. Picking up my walking stick, I hoof along.

Before walking into the village of Cacabelos, I see a hill. Hiking up to the hilltop, I walk deeper into the rain and the mist. As I look up, a magnificent rainbow appears. The vibrant colors form a perfect arch. Both ends of the rainbow stretch across the region. I stop for a little while and gaze upon it. I stand in awe. Cool misty water touches my face. I am refreshed. I close my eyes. A pleasant tingling sensation goes through my body. This is a feeling of ecstasy.

"I am in exactly the place I need to be," I thought to myself. Opening my eyes, I begin to walk once again. The rainbow is with me until I reach the Cacabelos. I believe I am not alone on this journey. Something greater than I is with me.

Heading in the direction of the Cúa River, I arrive at the village of Cacabelos. This village dates back to the tenth century. In earlier times, there were several hospices catering to the pilgrims. Today, not many exist. In the distance, I see a few friends standing near a bridge. They wave to me. As I walk toward them, the rainbow disappears. With a sigh of gratitude, I take a deep breath. I join my friends. I continue hiking with my friends. We walked through more vineyards.

"This is wine country," I said.

"Yes, look at all the vineyards. This is amazing," a friend said in delight.

As we walk into the small village of Pieros, one of my friends sees a fruit tree next to a house. The fruit is hanging over the fence. He stops and looks curiously at the fruit.

"These are some type of oranges," he said as he touches the fruit.

Then a window opens. An elderly woman pops her head out the window. Startled, we jump back. She smiles and pulls some of the fruit from the tree. She gives each of us an orange. The woman smiles at us as we peel our oranges. The juices from the orange burst in my mouth.

"Thank you very much. This is delicious," I said bowing to the woman.

My friends agreed. The woman signals for us to take more oranges. I took another. I chose to slip it into my pocket, so that I will have something to refresh and energize me later.

I am walking alongside a roadway on my way to Villafranca del Bierzo. The rain has stopped for the moment. Still wearing my poncho, I decide to leave it on until I reach Villafranca del Bierzo.

We have a large group walking in the same direction. I want to cross the highway to keep on walking. I stop before I cross over. I look left and right then left again. I could see a hiker walking in my direction. He looks as if he is in a hurry.

He is tall and thin. His dark loose curly hair rests above his shoulders and is blowing in the wind. He is wearing an olive green poncho with a red and white gingham shirt, khaki shorts, and hiking shoes. As he makes his way through the crowd, he looks at me. I could not help but stare back at him.

"Is he walking toward me? Who is this person?" I wondered to myself. As I am about to cross the roadway, the gentleman came directly up to me.

"Do you speak French?" he asked.

"No, I speak English. Why?" I answered.

"Do not cross the highway," he said.

"But I want to walk on the other side," I replied.

"Last week some folks were killed here. Be careful," he pointed out.

"Excuse me, but could you please repeat what you have just said?" I asked politely. The gentleman repeats again the news of the deaths. I became startled. This cannot be happening.

"Could this be true?" I asked myself. I turn to say something to the gentleman. To my surprise, he is gone. I could not find him. "Where did he go? Maybe he went down the way," I said softly. I looked left. He is nowhere in sight. I turn my head to the right. "Where is he?" I wondered in bewilderment. I could see a friend coming my way.

"Hello. I need to ask you something," I said anxiously.

"Sure ask away," she said.

I described the gentleman to her. "Have you seen such a man?" I asked.

"No, I have not seen the man you described," she answered. "Go and ask someone up ahead," my friend suggested.

"Thank you. I will," I replied. Then I turned and I began to walk again. I am thinking about the gentleman. "I did not imagine him. We had a conversation," I reassured myself.

Then I could see another friend up ahead. As I made my way up to him, I began to walk with him. "I need to ask you something," I said.

"What is it?" he asked.

I described the gentleman to him. "Did a gentleman walk this way? Have you seen him?" I asked.

"Sorry, but I have not seen any gentleman resembling the man you are asking about. Why?" he said.

Then I explained to him what had happened.

"When we get to Villafranca del Bierzo, we could ask the caretaker at the albergue. If anyone would know, it would be a caretaker?" my friend implied.

"Thank you," I said strangely.

Walking a few more kilometers, we followed the yellow marker into the village. My friends and I checked into the albergue at Villafranca del Bierzo early afternoon. After the caretaker stamped my credential, I inquired about if there was an accident last week.

"What is your question?" the caretaker asked.

"Was there an accident last week involving pilgrims? The accident would have been between Pieros and here?" I clarified.

The caretaker looked at me strangely. "No, there has not been an accident. We would know about something like this," he replied.

Then I gave details about the gentleman I came across earlier.

"If there was an accident, I would have heard about it," he said emphatically.

"Thank you for sharing this information," I said.

My friends and I looked at each other. We shrugged our shoulders, confused. "I am going to let this be for now. This is something I cannot answer," I decided.

"Yes, I agree," a friend answered.

"Now, let us go and find our bunks for the night," another friend suggested.

In the evening, I went to Saint James Church in the village. This church goes back to the eleventh or twelfth century. Behind the altar, a floor-to-ceiling work of art beautifully depicts a golden crown. The wooden pews are low and simple. Simplicity is the beauty in this church.

Sitting in the church for a little while, I feel at peace. After trekking today, everything seems to be still. My eyes are filled with tears. These tears are coming from feelings of forgiveness and joy. I ask God for forgiveness to make my wrongs right. In the house of God, I am filled with joy. When I feel filled up, I walked outside of the church.

As I am standing on the steps, I see a friend. She came up to me. "Would you like to join me for dinner? There is a small eatery here," she said with a smile.

"Yes, I would be delighted to join you," I accepted graciously.

We began to walk down a small narrow cobblestone pathway. Decorative black wrought iron balconies attached to the stone buildings are beautiful.

The eatery is not difficult to find. Seeing others ahead of us, we confirm that we are walking in the right direction. Stepping inside, we see more friends.

Messages

We sit down with them. We drink a lot of water. I order my favorite Spanish dish—vegetarian paella. This meal will fill me for tonight. My friend orders the same dish. As usual, the regional wine is served with the meal. Personally, I passed on the wine and gave my glass to a friend.

As we waited for our meal, one of our friends mentioned a bit of sad news.

"Another of our friends stopped walking because of a leg injury. This is sad," he said.

We looked at each other with care and concern. An injury could happen to anyone of us here. We say a little prayer for our friend.

After dinner, we all make our way back to the albergue. We hug and wish each other a Buen Camino.

Before falling asleep, I recapture my day. This journey takes me to places of adventure I would have never imagined. From early morning, the beauty of nature surrounds this region. To experience a beautiful rainbow today, misty rain, tasty oranges, and messages from strangers are delightful tidbits on this wonderful walk. I can hear sounds of laughter from other folks. They too, have their stories. One thing is for sure, this day is coming to an end.

Tomorrow awaits me.

Day 26 ~ La Faba

Grazing Land

Today I begin with a big bang. Trying to find my way out of Villafranca del Bierzo seems easy. For some reason I missed the Camino marker. Turning left instead of right I found myself walking through a long dark tunnel. At first, this looks scary. No yellow markers insight. Then I decided to turn around. Walking back through the tunnel, I could see the marker against a stone wall. Not far away, a couple flags me with their flashlight.

"How did I miss the marker?" I asked myself. I am not going to worry about. It is early in the morning, but I do need to be more watchful.

Crossing over the Burbia River relaxed me. Breathing in the morning moisture, I could feel myself being grounded to the earth. There are two paths to choose from this morning. The first path goes through a wooded area with a variety of trees along the way. The second path takes the hiker over, under, and alongside a river. The first path is a little longer than the second, but both paths connect at Trabadelo.

"Which path will I take today?" I pondered. Then I could feel a little nudge tug inside of me. I will take the second path. This way I will walk alongside the Valcarce River. Although the journey will not be tiring, I will be walking through a deep and narrow valley. I need to save my energy. Later today, I will climb a mountaintop heading toward O Cebreiro.

While walking beside the Valcarce River, I could hear the sound of water. Consciously pacing my footsteps keeps me in rhythm with the river. The crisp air smacks me on my face. The wind will keep me wide-awake and focused. Then the wind begins to pick up. All of sudden, a strong blustery gust zips through the valley. This valley is deep and narrow. Looking up at the sky, I can see clouds rolling in. I considered if I should bring out my poncho now or later. If it begins to rain, then I will put on my poncho.

After switchbacking across the roadway, I reach the small settlement of Pereje. In the eleventh century, a church and a hospital were built to help the pilgrims with their passage. Although the hospital is no longer here, the church remains.

Leaving Pereje brings me back to the Valcarce River. Once again, the wind picks up. Holding onto my hat, I continue my walk for another four kilometers. Trees crackled as gusts of wind blow them up through the valley. Walking against the wind is challenging. I must concentrate on taking one step at a time. I begin to smell chestnuts. The chestnut trees welcome travelers as they come into this village. I arrive at Trabadelo.

I notice some town folk walking about. I could smell honey. The folks here raise bees. With all of my attention on the aroma of the honey, and none on my steps, I lost my balance. Plop!

"My goodness, this is not happening," I said in surprise. Looking down I could only laugh aloud. "I am in a cow pie," I said with amusement.

Laughing so hard, tears of joy rolled down my face. How could I forget this is grazing land! I tried to shake the cow poop off my shoes. "What does this mean? Could any good come out of this mess?" I asked myself. "I have an idea. I will walk toward the river and put my feet in the water while still wearing my shoes. This way I will not need to take them off," I thought cleverly.

I did not want to stop here. The smell of cow poop started to waft up from my feet. I made my way out of the town. After walking just a little way, I came to a small stream. I see a rock near the stream. Walking over to the rock and carefully balancing myself I begin to rinse the heels of my shoes.

"Clean. No more cow poop," I observed. Taking a deep breath, I decided to stay until my shoes dried. "This is too funny," I said giggling.

Since I am sitting patiently, I decided to reach into my pocket and bring out the Pieros orange from yesterday. Each orange slice is sweet and juicy. This is delicious. After eating the orange, I felt new oomph to continue my walk.

Walking along the path, I reached the village of Ambasmestas. This tiny village has some remains of an old Roman road. From this village, I reconnected to the Valcarce River again. The river sounds again bring rhythm to my footsteps. I feel like dancing in the woods today. The birds make beautiful chirping sounds. Water, birds, and my humming carry me through the woods again today. This is simply charming.

Passing through the community of Ruitelán, I cross a bridge to get to Las Herrerías. This village is near a river. Since the tenth century, this village's industry has been iron and steel. Although the old foundry is no longer in operation, the structure remains. The architecture of the houses is interesting. Some houses have thatched roofs. Great! These houses are a beginning to indicate what is up ahead, especially O Cebreiro.

On the trail up to La Faba, the ground became steep and rocky. Walking with a group, we came upon cow traffic. As we are going up, the cows are coming down. The hikers split up. Some are on the left side and others on the right side of the roadway. I walked on the left side. An elderly man is herding his cows and he is guiding his donkey. The hikers stopped to let the man, his cows, and his donkey pass by.

Then one of the cows broke away from the herd. The cow walks toward me. I am still and calm. At the moment there is nowhere else I could go.

"What is this cow doing?" I asked. Her big brown eyes are fixed on me. She walks up to me. Then she begins to push me against the building with her face.

"Am I in your way?" I asked her.

With her large horns, she hooks my right arm. Immediately I became startled. Pain surges through me from the pressure of this massive beast. I quickly grab my arm. Tears began to fill my eyes.

"I am in your way. Sorry, I will move," I said aloud.

Then the herd passed. The cow proudly moved away from me to continue her walk. I could see the cow herder looking back at me. He looks sad about what has happened.

"Buen Camino," the elderly man shouted.

A gentleman behind me could see what had happened. "Are you all right?" he asked.

I held my arm to relieve the pressure.

"I am a doctor. Please let me look at your arm," the gentleman said.

I removed my rucksack. Taking off my jacket, I could feel my arm tighten. Looking at my arm, I could see the bruise instantly turning my skin shades of blue and green, and dark. My arm has already begun to swell. The doctor immediately took out his first aid kit. He applied an ointment to stop the pain and lessen the swelling.

"Thank you for doing this," I said in tears.

"You will be fine. No broken bones, but you will have a bad bruise," he said kindly. The doctor wrapped my arm to keep it firm.

"Will I be able to carry my rucksack?" I asked the doctor.

"You will, but you need to be careful. If the pain persists, take the rucksack off," the doctor suggested.

I carefully put on my jacket. Then the doctor helped me with my rucksack.

"Here, take this ointment with you. You may need it tonight and over the next couple of days," the doctor said.

"Thank you for your help today," I said feeling very sore.

"You are welcome. I am glad that I am here to help," the doctor replied.

As I began to climb to the mountaintop, I continue to feel the pain in my arm. My goal today is to walk up to O Cebreiro. This will be another five kilometers. I am at about 900 meters in altitude. Climbing up to O Cebreiro will be another 500 meters. I think not. La Faba is about one kilometer from here. I will stay overnight there.

Grazing Land

Seeing the road sign La Faba, I increase my pace. Tucked in the woods, on a mountain slope, sits an albergue. As I make my way up the steps, I can see the beauty around the albergue. After checking in, I walk to my bunk. Taking off my rucksack, I could feel some relief in my arm. Then taking off my jacket, I make my way to the showers. After removing the gauze from my arm, I ran cold water on it. This feels good. The bruising on my arm is a deep black and blue mark now.

After my shower, I walked down the steps to see a monument; the figure of Saint James. Made out of cast iron, Saint James is holding a stick, wearing open shoes, a cloak, and a hat. The monument is unique. Saint James has one foot on the ground and the other on a rock. He has his left hand stretched back with something in it. Staring at the monument, I could see a young bearded Saint James. He walks toward wind. His hat is flipped back to catch the breeze.

This area is serene. Here I am high in the mountains today. There are very few buildings around. Thick forest surrounds this albergue. Hikers will be passing by soon making their way to O Cebreiro. Although I will not reach O Cebreiro today, I am not worried. Holding my injured arm, I realize sometimes things happen for a reason. I do not know what the reason is today. Letting it be for now is the best I can do.

After a while, I could see a few hikers. Hands and hats are waving in the air. My friends are here. We greeted each other.

"Buen Camino," a friend said with delight. He squeezed my right arm.

"Ouch!" I winced in pain.

"What is this?" he asked.

I explained to my friends what had happened to me. "I hope my arm will be fine tomorrow. Stopping here to rest is the best for me. I need to allow my body to heal a bit, because I still need to reach the end of this walk," I said in determination.

My friends decided to stay overnight at the albergue. This is good. At least, I will not be lonely. Having the company of friends will take my mind off of my bruised arm.

Finding my way in the albergue, I walked to the living room. On a shelf, I could see a flashlight. I inquired about it.

"What are these things on this shelf for? Do they belong to someone?" I asked.

"Yes, they do belong to someone. The hikers left these things behind. Do you see something you would like?" the caretaker asked.

"Yes, I do. I see the flashlight," I replied.

The caretaker reached to the top shelf and brought it down. "Here it is. You may have it," the caretaker offered kindly.

"Thank you. I need to replace my flashlight," I said gratefully. I opened the flashlight. "Batteries come with it," I said quite pleased. Then the caretaker smiled and walked away.

I am in awe. This flashlight is sturdy. I will not need to think about light the rest of the journey. It is amazing how things work out over time. Keeping it simple is a priority in my life these days.

During the evening, we all gathered around the dining table. Other hikers found chairs to sit on in the dining room and living room. Sharing a meal and breaking bread shows kindness for each another. Our friendships continue to blossom along the way. After our meal, we clean up. Then we gather around to sing songs for the evening. Someone plays a flute. Peace, joy, and harmony fill the room. We are quiet. Eventually, I decide to get up to go to bed for the night. I wish everyone a Buen Camino and head to my bunk.

Once I settle in, I reflect on my events today. Stepping on cow poop this morning prepared me for the hard hitting cow this afternoon. This could have been awful. I am appreciative a doctor was standing near me when the mad cow appeared. As I hold my arm, I pray it will be fine in the morning. I also include in my prayers all who have injured themselves today. I wish for them enough inner strength and spirit to continue their journey. Yes, this walk may not seem easy, but in the end, the challenge will be worth it. I am beginning to feel its worth.

I am looking forward to tomorrow's hike. The boundary between León and Galicia is soon approaching. Galicia is the last region before reaching Santiago de Compostela.

Blackbirds

Today is August 17th. It is five o'clock in the morning and I can barely get out of my bunk. I did not sleep well last night. When everything became quiet in the albergue, my arm began to throb.

"I hope I will have enough energy for today," I whispered.

I realize how much worse this could have been and I give thanks. Being so close to the end of this journey, I vow that I will crawl if I have to. I am determined to finish the Camino.

"Look on the bright side. This time next week I will be walking to the finish line," I said to myself joyfully. After getting ready, I applied the ointment to my arm. This is soothing. Then I put on my jacket.

"Could I help you with your rucksack?" someone asked.

I turned and smiled. "Yes. Please do," I said to the gentleman.

"How is your arm today? I hope you will do well on your hike. Buen Camino," he said gently.

"My arm hurts, but I think I will be fine. Thank you for your help. Buen Camino to you as well," I said appreciatively.

Leaving the albergue at half-past five, I open the door to walk downstairs. As I made my way down, I could see many hikers camping out in the yard and in an open patio. Holding onto my new flashlight, I walked around sleeping bodies to get to the pathway. Who knows what time they came in last night or early this morning? Getting on the path, I looked back at the albergue. "I am happy to have stayed here last night," I nodded.

From La Faba to Triacastela will be twenty-six kilometers. Taking a deep breath to inspire myself, I begin trekking. Going uphill to O Cebreiro is challenging. The hike is steep, over rocks and hard ground. Glancing to the east, I see a beautiful sunrise. Pink ribbons appear in the sky. So far the weather is clear. I have reached Laguna de Castilla. Fantastic! Walking a little way, I came to a water fountain. It is time to refill my camelbak. The water is super cold.

Seeing what is around in the area, I realize I am leaving behind the region of León. From here, I will be entering into Galicia. This marks 152 kilometers before reaching Santiago de Compostela.

After a while, I feel as though I am walking in fog. I feel a shiver through my jacket. "Wow, this is getting nippy," I said chattering my teeth.

The crisp air keeps me awake. I take deep breaths of the clean air on this high mountaintop. As light peeks through the sky, I look down below to enjoy the picturesque view of mountains, hills, and valleys. I can see beautiful rolling terrain as if it is weaving over and under itself.

By seven o'clock, I arrived at O Cebreiro. Walking up a stone roadway, I see short stone markers with yellow arrows leading me into the village.

"This is astonishing. For sure, I cannot miss going through here," I said delighted. The village has primitive thatched-roof stone dwellings. In the ninth century, people from Celtic communities migrated here. The architectural design of these thatched-roof stone dwellings is enthralling.

I walked into the Santa María la Real Church. This village has a story. The Holy Grail that Jesus used at the Last Supper was hidden here in O Cebreiro. In the thirteenth or fourteenth century, a man walked through a snowstorm to O Cebreiro to attend Mass. At the moment he walked in the doorway the priest was consecrating the bread and wine. The priest was not pleased the man walked all the way for a piece of bread and wine. The bread and wine turned into flesh and blood.

As I walked into the museum, I could see a few friends. We chatted how incredible this place is. Then we walked over to the café to have something hot to drink.

"The weather up here is cold," I said trying to get warm.

"I agree with you. It is cold and this place is beautiful," a friend commented.

After warming up a bit, we walked together. I did not want to leave O Cebreiro and the warmth and comfort. Then I see a monument. It is the figure of a pilgrim. I could imagine the man walking through the wind. The pilgrim is holding onto his hat with his left hand. His jacket is flapping in the wind. He is carrying a walking stick. The pilgrim is standing on a rocky foundation. This pretty much sums up the terrain in this region.

As I walked downward, I turned several times to look back. It is as if I went back into time for a moment.

"I am not in a hurry today," I reminded myself. Walking one foot in front of the other, I slowly made my way down the rocky slope.

After walking eight kilometers, I pass through the villages of Liñares, Hospital da Condesa, and Padornelo. Slowly I continue descending, and then uphill again along a path on a mountainside. The forest gives shade along the way. Passing along meadows, the air is clean. I breathe deeply so that I can keep my balance. The sunlight feels good. Big white puffy clouds race across the sky in the wind. I am humbled by nature and her simple magnificence.

Arriving at Fonfría, I teamed up with some friends.

I could see an elderly woman. She wore a blue sweater over a brown dress with a red and white kerchief on her head. The woman is selling something—crepes.

"I am hungry," I said.

My friends and I stopped to eat. A local woman handed me a few crepes. She sprinkled powered sugar as a topping. As I bit into one of the crepes, the chocolate melted in my mouth.

"These are delicious," a friend said to the woman.

"Yes, this is tasty," I said nodding my head.

The woman smiled in delight. Then we started to hike again.

"Buen Camino," the woman said. We looked back at the woman and waved.

"Thank you. The crepes hit the spot," I said very pleased.

"It sure did," said another friend.

After walking a while the terrain became even rockier. The narrow path did not help to make it easier. We could hear bells.

"Bicycles are here today," I yelled. My friends and I jumped to one side. The three bicyclists zoomed by.

"Buen Camino," one of the riders said. In a flash, they disappeared.

Suddenly I feel an eruption in my stomach. "I am sorry, but you will need to walk without me. I need to take a timeout for Mother Nature," I said hurriedly.

Hands are waving in the air as if to say we will see you later. "Buen Camino," a friend said.

In a dash, I disappeared in the woods to relieve myself.

Hiking back on the trail, I continued to think about O Cebreiro. "The place is magnificent and is beyond what my little mind can absorb," I chuckled.

The trail is thick with bushes, flowers, and trees. I hear sounds of birds. I look up toward the sky. Three blackbirds soar above me. Taking a breather, I watch the blackbirds hovering above me. One of the birds decides to land. I walk in the direction of this blackbird. I became startled.

"Yesterday, I had a cow incident. Today, a blackbird," I said a little frighten. There is no one else on this trail. I cannot stay and wait to see what this bird will do. As I approach the blackbird it looked back at me. "Okay. I need to walk the trail," I said loudly.

Then I heard another sound. Two other blackbirds landed behind me. I firmly held my walking stick.

"Be not afraid. I am with you," my little voice inside me said.

I became calm. Getting closer to the blackbird, I passed by cautiously. Then I turned around. The three birds soared high into the air. Then I could feel plop, plop, and plop on my hat.

"This cannot be happening," I quivered in a low voice. Taking off my hat, I could see three bird droppings. "Cow poop yesterday and bird droppings today," I laughed. One thing is for sure out here I never know what to expect. I pinned my hat to the side of my rucksack. Stretching my sore arm, I reached for my second hat.

"Put on your hat. This should do it," I giggled. "Every day is a new surprise. There is never a dull moment out on the trail," I said.

When I reached the village of Biduedo, I could see some friends taking a break.

"Buen Camino," I said.

"Hello. You changed your hat," a friend observed.

"I met three blackbirds on the trail. They sent me a little gift as they flew above me. It is a long story," I said mischievously. As I said this, I turned to the side to show my hat. They began to laugh.

"This is the best story yet," a friend said jokingly.

"Surprising things do happen to you," another friend commented.

"Yes, I am attracted to surprises. It is all about cow poop and bird droppings. Today is not over yet," I said with a grin.

As I left the village of Biduedo, it was like a flume ride downhill. I passed through the villages of Filloval, As Pasantes, and Ramil heading toward Triacastela. Although the terrain is challenging, the mountainous area around here is captivating.

Trekking near Triacastela, I can see an elderly man wearing a brown hat, a white T-shirt, and black trousers. He is sitting on a chair. Next to him are walking sticks. These sticks are different shapes and sizes. As I get closer, the man stands up. He brings out a stick.

"One euro," the man shouted.

"I will buy it," someone said.

I turned around to see my friends walking behind me. One bought two sticks.

The man smiled. "Buen Camino," he said.

As we walked away we turned and said, "Buen Camino."

From the top of a hill, the view of Triacastela, which means three castles, is spectacular. This is a postcard view. The quaint village is nestled in a lush deep valley.

"I will stay here tonight," I decided aloud. My friends also decided to stay here. I slowly make my way into the village. I stopped by the parish church, Saint James. The church is built of stone blocks. An archway leads into the church. The tower has the coat of arms of the three castles. A statue of Saint James is embedded on one of the sides below the church tower. The church bells are in arches in the tower. A crown rests on top the tower with a cross above it.

In the village, I found the albergue. As the caretaker stamped my credential, she mentioned there would be Mass tonight at the church. After finding my bunk, I sat down and gently removed my rucksack. This feels good. I survived today. I will find a market to buy food for tonight and tomorrow.

Standing outside the albergue, I heard someone call me. Looking around I could see someone waving. It is a friend. I walked up to her. Together we walked to the market.

Returning to the albergue, we prepared our meal. This evening we are having pasta and salad. Other folks came to join us. There is enough for everyone.

After dinner, we walked over to the church. Tonight is special. I read a scripture in English from Luke 24:15-19. I also read a Solemn Blessing. One of my friends read in her native language. In the end, the priest blessed the pilgrims. This has been an extraordinary day.

From here, it will be 126 kilometers to Santiago de Compostela. The days are going by quickly. I am almost to the end.

Day 28 ~ Barbadelo

Crossroads

Just before the crack of dawn, I am up and ready for another day. Leaving Triacastela, I have two hiking options. The first option is slightly shorter than the second. However, hiking will be at a higher elevation. The difference between the two options is about four kilometers. Both paths will connect at the city of Sarria. The second option goes to Samos where there is a famous monastery. It is one of the oldest monasteries in Spain.

Leaving the albergue, I trek through the village in mist and fog. My face feels damp and wet. I reach into the side of my rucksack and bring out my gloves.

"This is cold. I am smart to be wearing my gloves this morning," I said shivering.

Although it is cold, the beauty is surreal. The village is nestled in a valley. It is quiet. As I look in front of me, I can see a few houses. Lights are on. Smoke from the chimneys swirl skyward. I can feel myself breathing.

As I fill my lungs with crisp air, I can see my exhale. I humor myself thinking I am like a chimney this morning. The winding roadway takes me out of the village.

I am standing at a crossroad. "Do I take option one or option two?" I asked myself.

Although I would like to take option two, option one is the route I decide to take. As much as I would like to hike option two, I am in strong enough condition to hike option one. Hiking up the mountain, I begin to breathe hard and harder. My climb will be 350 meters up to a mountain peak. Then it will be downhill passing through several villages.

In a moment of reflection, I think back to when I first started this walk. The walk has been beautiful from day one. Simple things I had taken for granted are important to me now. For example, I will appreciate taking a bath. To have water run down my filthy body is a cleansing. I have learned over these past weeks that washing clothes by hand is possible. My rucksack and I are one. Of course, my walking stick is my support. It carries me when I feel I cannot take another step. Each time I put the stick in front it pulls me one step closer to my daily destinations. Last but not least, my walking shoes trekking 500 miles.

As I climb uphill, I can see the first light of the day. This is invigorating to my being. The incredible sunrise beams and burst light everywhere. I have crossed over mountains, hills, rivers, and strea⊃ roughout this journey. Medieval bridges throu⊃ ⊃ walk connect to cultivated lands, roads, an⊃ ⊃ along the way. I am thankful for another day t⊃ ⊃e.

Trekking through several village⊃ ⊃way, I could not help but think about the ⊃ ⊃ my life. I believe these crossroads have b⊃ ⊃re on this walk. This is a walk I never imagi⊃ ⊃ course, I knew about this historical trail fo⊃ chose to do it one day when I retire from wo⊃ adventurer, traveling is becoming my favorite p⊃ ⊃.

This is the child inside of me that always wants to discover. As a child, I would dream of living in faraway places. Learning about different countries and cultures excites me. As I got older and married, this dream got push to the back burner of my life. My children and husband became the dream I lived. Then my children grew up. After my divorce, I was left with only myself. This became my cross. I took up my cross. I embraced my cross.

Embracing my pain and suffering has brought me to walk the Camino. Through my difficulties and despairs in my life, I did not lose heart. Today, my cross is lifted. My burden is light. I keep reflecting on Jesus' words in John 14:6, "I am the way, and the truth, and the life." Focusing on Jesus leads me on the straight and narrow path.

Living and working in Germany has helped me to heal my pain. I became like a little child again. Like a child, I feel loved again. When I now think back, the crossroads in my life have brought me here. I need to heal. If I am to love again, I need to know I am well inside. Every day I feel a little better. Of course, there are days when I do not feel good. Over time, I grow stronger. I am letting time be my best healing source.

Crossing a bridge over the Sarria River, I stand in awe. The town sits on a hill. There are several churches in this town. The yellow marker brings me to the Church of The Convent of Mary Magdalena. Walking inside, I see that the worship space is illuminated by a high altar. The arch dome reaches high above the floor. I sit comfortably.

"Do I want to stay here tonight? Do I have the strength to continue walking today?" I asked myself these simple questions.

Then I felt the urge to walk a bit further, a little beyond Sarria. With a deep breath, I stood up. "I will walk a little more today," I said. Stepping outside of the church, I passed a cemetery.

Passing the town, I reach the Ponte Áspera Bridge, commonly used to cross the Celeiro River. The markers take me to a railway crossing and a stream, which lead me to the woods again. As I walk a few more kilometers, I can feel the sun is hot today. I realize it will prudent for me to stop somewhere fairly soon. I do not want to exhaust myself. The hamlet of Vilei is up ahead, however, I still have enough energy to continue.

Hiking over rolling hills, I ascend to higher ground. The stone houses in the hamlets in this region are small in numbers. Most of the folks are farmers. The farmlands are lush with vegetables and fruit trees. Walking along the narrow roads, raised corncribs are visible.

By early afternoon, I see a sign for Barbadelo. I can see a church tower in the village. This is the parish church of Saint James. Across the roadway on the corner of a grassy area is an old white house with a large porch. The house sits on the pathway. Walking over to the house, I could not help but notice it is an albergue. I can see some folks sitting on the steps waiting for the albergue to open.

I see hands waving. "Oh my, I see some friends," I said smiling. Picking up my pace, I walked over to them. "Hello. Buen Camino," I said with delight.

"Buen Camino to you," a friend replied.

"Are you staying here tonight?" I asked.

"Yes. Another friend and I will be staying here," she answered.

"I will stay here tonight as well," I replied.

Since the albergue is closed, I took off my rucksack and put it in line. Then I stretched my tired body. As I am walking down the stairs, I see a little shop.

"I am hungry," I said.

At the shop, I picked up fruits and vegetables for tonight and tomorrow. Making my way back, I see that the albergue has opened. I picked up my rucksack and checked in for the night.

My bunk for the night is next to a window. A friend has her bunk next to mine. I strolled over to the showers to freshen up. After a hardy day's walk, it is good to feel clean again. I looked at my arm. Although the pain has subsided, the bruise reminds me of the cow that went wild. The pains in my knee have been much less. The terrain has conditioned my body.

During the evening, I strolled over to the church. Before walking inside, I notice two old stone crosses at the entrance. The three dimensional nave welcomes folks. The tower is on one side with an arched window that overlooks the village. The façade of the church stands tall. To the side of the church is a cemetery. Looking at some of the headstones, people have been buried here a very long while. Once inside of the church, I found myself feeling cold. There are no windows to look outside. These stonewalls hold the chill. Finding a wooden pew, I sit in reflection.

Then the priest came into the church. "We will have Mass," the priest announced.

"Thank you," I replied.

Then a few minutes later others came into the church. After Mass, the priest gave us a pilgrim's blessing. I closed my eyes and sat in silence. A warm gentle feeling touched my cheek. I reached to touch it. My hand instantly became warm as well. For a moment, my hand rested on my cheek. I am not alone. This is special.

I reflected on the words of Jesus in Matthew 28:20, "I am with you always." I believe this. Something stirred inside of me. Tears flowed down my face. I am weeping tears of joy. "Thank you, Lord. You are kind and merciful," I whispered.

Then the priest came to us and gave us a tour of the church. "The church was built in the twelfth century. This church has one of the oldest bell towers in the world," the priest explained.

I walked up stairs to peek inside the bell tower. "Wow, it is dark. This is amazing," I said softly.

Walking back to the albergue, I could see a little dog sitting on the steps. As I approached him, his little head popped up. I sat next to him. Then a friend came along and sat next to us.

"Little dog, how many pilgrims have you seen?" I asked.

"Woof, woof, woof," the dog barked.

This amazed me. "Do you understand what I am saying," I asked the dog. Then the dog put his head on my lap and whimpered.

"Well I take it you have seen a lot of pilgrims come through here," I said enjoying myself. The dog lifted his head and looked directly at me. His big brown eyes shone crystal clear.

A friend heard my conversation with the dog. As she sat next to us, she admired the dog as well. Spontaneously, I called the dog Puppy Camino. Then I introduced my little friend.

"Puppy Camino meet another friend," I said. The dog turned his head and stared at my friend.

"I am happy to meet you Puppy Camino," she cooed as she took the dog's paw. We laughed.

After dinner, I walked to my bunk. As I stretched out in my bunk, I looked out the open window. I hear footsteps. It is hikers walking pass the albergue. I can see three of them chatting and laughing.

"It is dark. Where are you staying tonight?" I asked softly.

"We are walking as far as our strength will take us," one of the hikers replied.

"Buen Camino," I said.

"Buen Camino to you and good night," another hiker said.

When the hikers left, there is stillness. The stars are shining brightly in the sky tonight. I can see why the hikers would choose to walk at night. It is cooler.

Crossroads

Today has been a day of crossroads for me; crossroads on the journey and in my life. I feel reconnected. I am not afraid. A little breeze comes through the window. It feels good. Sometimes words cannot describe the way I feel. It is during moments like this that I am silent.

100 Kilometers

Today is Sunday, August 19th. I am excited this morning. Ready to take off, I walk down the steps of the albergue. I feel something warm brush against my leg. As I look down to see what it is, I stop. It is Puppy Camino.

"Hey buddy. Good morning to you, too. It is good to see you this morning," I said feeling chipper. I bend over to pet him and he presses his head against my leg again.

"I have to go now. Puppy Camino go back home. Your master will be looking for you," I said softly. Then I pick him up and held him. I run my fingers through his fur. His body is warm and his heart is beating fast.

"I cannot take you with me," I whisper in his ear. Suddenly, Puppy Camino looks at me and licks my face.

"Woe to you. Is this a going away kiss? If so, I will hold you a little longer. It will be my farewell hug to you," I said. Holding him tighter, I do not want to let him go, but I must. Putting Puppy Camino on the ground, I tap him lovingly on the head.

"Take care, buddy," I say somewhat sadly. Attempting to get on my way again, I hear a whining sound.

"Good-bye," I said firmly.

"Woof, woof, woof," Puppy Camino barked insistently.

"Does this dog understand the meaning of good-bye?" I wondered aloud. I turned a last time to look back at him. He slowly turned away and walked back to the albergue. "I think I have made a new friend," I thought, quite pleased about it all.

The walk this morning is on hard surface. This is good. I make my way through small villages. These villages are lined up one right after another. Beautiful flowers in purple, yellow, pink, orange, and green are in bloom. I do not feel I am hiking now. This is more like a stroll through a park. This is a pleasant way to start my day. The scent of the flowers is delicious. I am delighted. As I take in deep breaths, I sneeze briefly. I bless myself as I drink in this pure and rich experience.

I have reached Mogarde. At last, I see a vertical stone marker. It reads K 100, which means 100 kilometers. I dance for joy. My hands are stretched out. I begin twirling in a circle. My head is bent back and my eyes see the sky.

"Yes, there are only 100 kilometers left on the journey to Santiago de Compostela. This is cool! I have reached another milestone," I shouted. I need to take a picture of the stone marker. As I got closer, I became disappointed.

"What, I do not believe it. Graffiti! This cannot be," I exclaimed. I decided to wait. Maybe the next stone marker will be clean. A walk-run pace is now my plan. Then I felt something pull me.

"Slow down speedy. Not so fast," a voice whispered.

"What is wrong with me?" I need to save my energy. Then I realized I still have ninety-nine kilometers yet to finish. Soon I heard sounds. As I turned, I could see little lights.

"Hello," I said in excitement.

"Good morning," someone replied.

"Have you seen the K 100 stone marker?" I asked in delight.

"Yes, we have seen the marker," another voice commented.

"I am standing at K 99," I said cheerfully.

"Wait up for us. We will be there shortly," the voices answered.

This will give me time to admire this beautiful marker. I reached into my jacket and took out my camera. I touched the marker gently. "I am so glad to see you," I said filled with joy.

Then I bent over to kiss the shell that is carved into the top of the marker. Beneath the shell, posted in orange, are the letters K 99. At the lower right corner is inscribed Diputacion Provincial Lugo. The marker is embedded in a rock. Green vines grow around the stone marker. I realize I am getting closer to the end. To see something like this is wonderful and greatly encouraging.

I realize these are my last days on this journey. The many mountains, hills, and valleys bring joy to me. This hike is worth it all.

Staring at the marker, I reflect back on the last few weeks of this journey. The message is clear in my mind. Deep within me the call to do this walk is important. I need to cleanse from my old to my new self. In doing so, I detached myself from the world. This journey is slowly transforming me.

Countless aches, pains, and blisters plagued me in the beginning. All of this helped to shed the old in me. As time went on somehow the pains subsided. Then new skin appears. I am anew. Walking back through the past brings me to the present. It is as if I am a caterpillar in a cocoon. As it dries and cracks my wings begin to break through. A butterfly springs forth and flies away. A caterpillar transforms into a butterfly. This is how I feel. Once trapped, now I am free.

Finally reaching Portomarín, I stop to look around. A modern bridge connects two valleys and the old town of Portomarín. Today, the Belesar Reservoir covers the old town. As I begin to cross the bridge, I picture what it might have been in the old city. The houses clustered around the town center. Roads led into and out of the area. Hospices for the pilgrims are buried here.

When the reservoir is low, like today, we can see parts of the old town resting beneath the water. I stopped in the middle of the bridge to gaze about. Thinking an old city is directly beneath amazes me. In time of drought, the ruins of the old city surface.

Crossing the bridge, I see steps leading up to the Chapel of Las Nieves. An arch from the old bridge was used to build the chapel. As I begin to climb the stone steps, I feel how steep it is to the top. Leaning over to the side, I see the arch from the old Roman bridge. Once I am at the top, I turn to see the direction from which I came from.

"Wow, this is quite amazing," I said in awe. Passing the chapel, I make my way into the town square.

"Hello," I said in excitement. I see some folks I know. Heads turn and hands wave in the air.

"Are you staying here tonight?" I asked.

"The albergues are full," a friend replied. He did not look too happy. Just as we thought, the closer we get to Santiago de Compostela the harder it will be to find a place.

"We are planning to go to another village. Do you want to walk with us?" he asked.

"Sure. I would be delighted," I accepted.

As I leave Portomarín with my friends, once again I appreciate the beautiful landscape. The vegetation near the water is full of life. I am leaving this fascinating town. I could have enjoyed spending the night here. It is almost noon. I hope it will not be difficult to find a place.

Once again, I cross a footbridge over the Belesar Reservoir. Walking to the village of Gonzar will be another eight kilometers. Getting there in the afternoon will be fine. The surface road goes along a stream. I enjoy the pleasant sounds as I continue on with my friends.

Making a turn, I see a stone marker. This time it is marked K 89. My strength picks up. "Just think, in a few days I will reach the end of this journey," I said. Then something came over me. I feel a little sad. "Why am I feeling like this?" I asked myself. I need to feel happy and shout with joy.

Having this adventure has helped me to escape for a little while. I will return with a different outlook about my life. I will be healed from the pain and suffering I have endured over the last decade. My burden will be lifted. I will be more humble. To see life with new perspective will be my reward. My eyes will have broader lenses instead of narrow tunnel vision.

Here I am walking through the forest. On both sides of the road are pine trees. I feel the warmth of the sun. I look up toward the sky at the sunlight beaming through the trees. There is no time to feel gloomy.

"Feeling sad makes me feel trapped. There is more to life than to feel sad. No sadness only joy," I shout. More feelings surged from within me. "I was lost, but now I am found. Leaving, I am returning. Even with my slip-ups in life, I am loved," I sing out with joy.

Walking out of the forest the sun radiates through my body. I feel warm all over. As I look ahead, I can see my friends in the distance. After passing cornfields and trees, I reach a little village, Toxibo. The farming here is abundant. Little houses come together in this quaint place.

As I take a sip from the camelbak, I begin to feel hungry. Reaching into my pocket, I bring out a piece of bread to munch on. "Food tastes better when I have less. How much do I need if I do not have a lot?" I ponder. I feel gladness and faith knowing I have only enough for today. Tomorrow will come later.

Little streams are along the paths today. I travel from one stream to another until finally into the little community of Gonzar, where I team up with my friends again.

"Is there an albergue here?" I asked.

"Yes, they do have a few bunks left," a friend reported.

"Wonderful. After walking twenty-eight kilometers today, I will stay here," I replied.

The caretaker at the albergue stamped my credential. He pointed in the direction of the bunks.

"Thank you," I said.

"You are welcome. We have only two bunks left," he replied.

"This is cutting it close," I thought. I picked up my rucksack and high-tailed it over to claim my bunk.

After freshening up, I washed my clothes. The wind started to pick up. "This is a good sign. My clothes will dry in a short time," I said.

Leaving the albergue, I walk down a roadway. I see a little church. The doors are locked. "I guess there is no priest in this village. No priest, no Mass," I said feeling a little gloomy. "Ah, there is a bench. I will scoot over and sit."

Looking around the village, I could see a stone cross in the middle of the square. Then an elderly woman dressed in a pink top with a green, blue, and pink-checkered apron, and blue shoes came walking toward me. She smiles. Then she motioned me to follow her. The woman takes me to a little store.

"Thank you," I smiled at her graciously. With a big grin, she smiled back.

"No need looking for a store. I think the store came to me," I mused. After picking up a few things for dinner and tomorrow, I make my way back to the albergue. Sharing a meal with friends is a delight.

"This cannot get any better," I thought to myself with much gratitude.

Day 30 ~ Melide

Craziness

My alarm goes off at five o'clock in the morning. "Rise and shine! Today is a new day," I said wide-eyed and a bushy tailed. Walking to the restroom, I could hear whispering. Thinking I am the first in line to freshen up, there are actually three other women.

"Good morning," I said cheerfully.

"Good morning to you," two women replied. The third woman looks as if she is still asleep.

I am ready to do this hike, but I have a hunch today will be a long journey. I am glad I slept well and had turned in early last night. My hiking will determine how well rested I truly am. Putting on my shoes, jacket, rucksack, and hat, I reach for my walking stick. Stepping outside of the albergue, others are gearing up as well. We are headed in the same direction today. We look as if we are entering a race to find a treasure.

As I begin to walk, some of the guys passed me in a flash. I feel like a tortoise. My rucksack is my shell.

My little head pops in and out when there is excitement. Then my head stretched.

"Bells are ringing. Bicycles are on the trail," I said with surprise. Moving quickly to the side of the trail, I counted five bicycles zoom by. I thought about how dark it is. The bicycle lights shine brightly. This is good. I do not have a problem with bicyclists this morning. They give me more light for what is up ahead.

My nose itches in the crisp air. I begin sneezing like crazy. As I sneeze, there is an echo way up through the trail. I brought out tissue and blew my nose long and hard. "There this should do it," I thought to myself. I could not remember if I had ever sneezed like that before.

"Keep focus. Do not go off track today," I laughed loudly.

Then all of sudden I hit a rock. Bump, bump and bump. I could feel my body falling to the ground. "No, this cannot be happening," I shouted. My flashlight flew out of my hand. "My goodness. It is dark. Where is my light?" I screeched.

"Be calm. Do not fear," a little voice inside me said.

Pulling myself together, I began to look around for my flashlight. To the side of the trail I could see a little beam of light. Then I walked over and picked up my flashlight.

"This is crazy. The light is still working," I said. Flashing my light around to see if I dropped anything helped to calm my nerves I spotted the rock I tripped over. It looked more like a boulder than a rock. Then I dusted myself off as I walked away. I could feel the dirt all over me.

"Wow, that was a strange fall," I said feeling upset. "Thank goodness this is not any worse. I would have had to wait for the next person to show up to find me." At the moment I am not feeling any pain. Maybe later on I will feel hurt. Once again, I reminded myself to keep focus.

As the sunlight brightens the sky, I can see my surroundings. There in front of me is a stone cross. I walk there to sit for a minute. When I reached the cross, I grabbed it. I held onto it for dear life. Tears began to flow like a running river. I became silent. I gave thanks for my life and that I am still okay and able to continue.

I have arrived at Os Lameiros. Looking at the cross more closing, I could see a Madonna with Child. This cross is different from all of the others I have seen on the trail. My tears slowly streamed down my face. I hugged the cross again. After the craziness this morning, I am glad to be here. Then I sat on one of the steps below the cross. I sipped my water. Reaching into my pocket, I brought out an apple. I began to eat it. This calmed my uneasiness. After eating my apple, I stood up and slowly trekked along.

Walking along a stone pathway, I came upon beautiful green trees. The sun shines through the tree branches. The shade is consistent along the way. It is cool for now. Later it will become warmer.

Climbing up to Alto do Rosario, I can see many oak trees. They are lovely. As I reach the summit, I can see other mountains in plain view. Descending downward, I see a stone marker indicating K 66.5. I do not need to think about the distance anymore. It is encouraging to see markers showing how many kilometers to walk. Soon I hear shouts and laughter. As I turn, I see it is some friends.

"Good day! Where are you headed today?" a friend asked.

"Well, I think I will go as far as Leboreiro. If the albergue is full, then I will trek until I find a place to stay overnight," I replied.

"Can we walk together?" another friend asked.

"Of course, why not. I wished I had someone earlier this morning," I answered. I explained to my friends about my little mishap. "Thank goodness I did not break any bones when I fell," I said.

"Yes, we are too close to the end of this journey," a friend mentioned.

"Sometimes close can seem far away," I commented.

The three of us teamed up and continued our hike. We paced ourselves so that no one would lag behind.

As we walk, I keep just a bit behind my friends. One friend began to sing. Before we knew it, all three of us are humming and singing along. I look up at the sky. The white puffy clouds are streaming across. Then I could see three clouds.

"Aha, this could be us," I said aloud.

"What could be us?" a friend asked.

"Look up at the sky. Three puffy clouds are just like us trekking along. Use your imagination and you will see," I said.

She looked up at the sky. "You are absolutely right. Here we are three pilgrims and three clouds trekking in the same direction on the same road. Where are these clouds headed?" she asked.

"They are not going where we are going," another friend replied.

"Ah, we do not know this," I commented. We laughed and continued singing with merriment.

"I am hungry. I am having a lunch attack," a friend said.

"Well, we are here in Palas de Rei," another friend replied. "Perhaps we could have lunch somewhere around here."

"Let us buy something and eat outside of the town. It would make our way to Leboreiro seem shorter," a friend said.

"That sounds cool. We can do that," I agreed. Being in sync, we are able to easily find a little market and pick up some food. As I walked outside of the market, I saw an interesting little building.

"I am going to check out this building. Please wait for me. I will not be long," I said.

"Go ahead. We will wait for you," a friend replied.

As I walked into the building, I looked around. "Hum, this looks like an official building," I whispered. Then a woman walked up to me.

"Hello, I am a hiker. Could you please tell me the name of this building?" I asked.

"Yes. It is the *concello*, a town hall. Do you have a credential?" she asked. Then she picked up her stamp.

"Yes, I do. Here it is," I replied. She stamped my credential. "Thank you very much," I said delighted. The woman smiled.

"I have two other friends. I think they may want to have their credentials stamped as well," I said.

"Have them come by. I could stamp their credentials," she replied.

Getting back to my friends, I told them about the town hall. They walked over and the woman stamped their credentials. We thanked the woman. She smiled at us.

"Buen Camino," the woman said.

"Have a good day ma'am," I answered.

As we began to depart the town, we could see the church, San Tirso. The façade of the church is decorated with shells. It is unique. We also stop to have our credentials stamped at the church.

My hunger pangs become stronger. "Is it already time for lunch?" I asked.

"Yes," my friends replied.

We found a quiet grassy place and shared our lunch. The sun helps us out by staying behind the clouds. It is not too hot. We make sandwiches and eat fruit. After lunch, we rest for a little while.

"This is a beautiful day," I said joyfully.

"Yes, it is hard to imagine we did not find an albergue yet," a friend said in a sullen voice.

"It is time we get our butts moving if we want to find a place tonight," another friend suggested.

"I agree," I said soundly. We pick up our tired bodies and put on our rucksacks. Walking at a snail's pace we look at each other and burst into laughter.

"This is why we eat when we reach an albergue. It becomes harder to pick up the pace after lunch," we said together laughing. We marched our way to the next village in a single line.

As we reach the village of Leboreiro, we find ourselves standing in front of a church, Santa María. Although this village goes back to the twelfth century, the church has been rebuilt in the eighteenth century. This church has a story. One night at a fountain, a glowing light shined. Some of the villagers noticed the light. While digging up the ground, the villagers found a statue of a lady. The villagers placed the statue on the altar in the church. In the morning, the statue would disappear. Re-digging the same place in the ground, the statue was found again. The church is dedicated to the lady. The statue remains in the church today.

Stepping outside, we could see others walking into an albergue. No sooner did they walk in then they walked back out.

"This albergue is full," someone said. My friends and I looked at each other.

"Next village," I suggested.

"I guess so," a friend replied.

"Oh well if push comes to shove we do have the stars, moon, and sky," I said.

"Indeed we do," a friend remarked.

Walking five more kilometers, we reach the village of Furelos. We cross over the Furelos River on a medieval bridge with four arches and then descend into the village. I stop in the middle of the bridge to look at the scenery. The water reflects the green trees and enhances the beauty. I think of the many hikers who have journey across this very bridge. Now, I am one of them.

Once again, all the albergues are full. As we leave Furelos, I turned to look back at the village. I take three deep breaths drinking in the beauty of this village.

If there were room here, I would have loved to spend the night. Turning myself around, I make my way out of this village.

After a while, the town of Melide appears. Long ago, this town is known to have been of importance for pilgrims. It had several hospitals. The hospitality of the townspeople helped folks making their pilgrimage to Santiago de Compostela.

I see an albergue. As my friends and I make our way over, we see people walking outside. "There are only a few bunks left," someone said.

"Thank you," I replied.

"We have a place to stay tonight," a friend said softly.

Holding our hands, we skip into the albergue. Our credentials are stamped. This is good news.

Today has been long and crazy. I walked thirty-one kilometers. Now I have a bunk to rest my drained body. I make my way to the showers. Life is good.

Day 31 ~ Santa Irene

Rocky Bridge

I am wide-awake this morning. Standing outside of the albergue, I am ready to take off. Feeling a little stiff from yesterday, I gradually move forward and begin to stretch out a bit. I am getting closer to Santiago de Compostela. The morning feels good. Walking among trees, I hear birds chirping. I imagine these birds saying, "Look a pilgrim is on her way to Carballal. Buen Camino."

In the distance, I see little lights flashing. It seemed like a signal of some sort.

"What is going on?" I asked no one in particular. Unexpectedly, I hear footsteps behind me. As I turned and pointed my light, I see a person covering his face. Clearly it is a male. He nearly tripped over me.

"You scared me," I exclaimed loudly.

"I am sorry. Could you share your light with me? I am walking without a light this morning," the young man said.

"Sure, I can share my flashlight with you. Please do not walk so close to someone like that. You could give a person a heart attack," I suggested.

"Where are you from?" I asked.

"I am from France," he said.

"What do you do?" I asked the young man.

"I am a medical student on school break. This is why I am here walking the Camino. What do you do?" he asked.

"I am on vacation for a couple of weeks. Walking the Camino is something I have always wanted to do. So I am here and now I have made a new friend this morning. Meeting you is both interesting and surprising," I said. Up ahead, I see more flashlights.

"Be careful. There is a rocky bridge over a stream is flowing rapidly," a voice yelled from across the way. Within an instant I could see the bridge directly in front of me.

"You go first, I will be behind you," the young man said.

"Thank you. I am not good at crossing rocky bridges," I said a little nervously. Then a flash came into my mind reminding me of the thunder, lightning, and mud slide a few weeks ago. Everything looks fine as I begin to cross the bridge. Darkness is beginning to fade into light a little. Sunrise will be soon.

"How are you doing?" the young man asked.

"As good as I can be," I said softly. Then I slipped on a big rock. "Oops. I think I am going to fall," I said with fear. I could feel myself falling, when, in the nick of time, a hand pulled me back.

"You are not going to fall. I have your back," the young man said.

"Thank you, kindly," I said with gratitude.

"Do not thank me yet. We are not across the bridge," he commented.

As I continue across the bridge, I feel the water from the stream ooze into my shoes. It is slushy. "Yuck! These are slippery rocks," I yelled. With my walking stick, I keep prodding my way across.

"Hang in there. I think we are almost to the other side," the young man suggested.

"I sure hope so because I am running out of energy. The water keeps rising. It is pulling me sideways. This is not a good time to go downstream," I said chattering. By now the water is up to my knees. Carefully, I continue to walk step by step. I could see some figures in a distance.

"Can you run across?" a voice shouted from the other side.

"No, I cannot run across. The water is too high. It is up to my knees," I replied.

"Take it slowly," the voice said.

"Do not be afraid. I am with you," my inner voice whispers.

"Please stay with me. Do not abandon me," I prayed softly. My arms began to feel stronger. I pick up my feet and walk forward. "I am not afraid. I will walk across to the other side," I said in a strong voice.

"What did you say?" the young man asked.

"I can do this because I have the strength," I replied.

"Good because we are almost there," he said.

The water is lower now. I see trees and a grassy area. "I think we have crossed over to the other side," I said with glee. Safely reaching the river bank, I turned around. The young man gave me a big smile.

"Yes, here we are past the danger," the young man shouted. "We did it! Thank you for your light this morning," he said.

"I need to thank you for your encouragement and support crossing this rocky bridge," I replied gratefully. We hugged one another. "Take care. Buen Camino," I said cheerfully.

As the young man walked away, my heart went with him. He is my hero for today. He turned around and waved good-bye. I felt sad and happy at the same time. Our friendship lasted for a short while, but at a crucial time.

Over to the side, I could see a few travelers. "You made the crossing safely," someone said.

"Yes. Someone special helped me across," I said in a heartfelt voice. I continued my walk in silence. The others walked in front of me. I am particularly grateful this morning.

Walking through deep valleys, I continue to cross small rivers along the way. The trail today includes hiking uphill and downhill throughout these valleys. Tall eucalyptus trees give shade along the path. Keeping my feet solidly on the ground, I continue to hike with strength and courage.

From a nearby village, the smell of cornbread fills the air. I inhale the fresh aroma. My stomach starts to rumble. I do not see anywhere or anyone selling cornbread. The smell is coming from the houses. Sipping water from my camelbak filled my tummy, so I trekked on.

I arrived at Ribadiso just over the Iso River. Crossing this bridge, I feel as though I have gone back in time. Although this bridge has been rebuilt several times, the original crossing dates back a long time ago. Taking my time, I imagine pilgrims making their way across this very bridge. I blink my eyes, marveling that it is me making the crossing. I feel a little disoriented. As I think of the many that have crossed here, I have a renewed desire to go across.

Finally, I reach Arzúa. My nose is tickling.

"What is this smell?" I asked. Taking a deep breath, I recognize the scent. "Aha! This smells like cow manure," I said laughing to myself.

From a little hilltop, I see a perfect view of Arzúa. The town is clustered on a hill. Crops of all sorts grow here. However, this is primarily dairy land. Walking through the town, I smell cheese everywhere. Stopping at one of the markets, I bought a wedge of cheese and a piece of bread to satisfy my appetite. As I bite into the bread and cheese, I salivate so boldly that it dribbles down the side of my mouth.

"This is delicious," I said savoring each bite. I sip water to wash it down.

By noon I reached Calzada. Without notice, an attack from Mother Nature catches me by surprise. "I think it must be the cheese. Is there a restroom somewhere?" I asked frantically.

Then I see a little café. A cleaning woman with her mop and buck has closed the women's side for cleaning. I look at her and she looks back at me. My face shows my distress.

"Please let me go into the restroom," I pleaded with praying hands. She takes pity on me. With one hand, she opens the men's restroom.

"May I go in?" I asked. She lets me into the men's restroom. "Thank you," I said expressing that I am in dire straits. I hope that she is keeping a lookout for me. When I finished, I stepped outside feeling great relief. The cleaning woman comes out from the women's restroom and stares at me.

"Thank you very much," I said appreciatively.

"Buen Camino," the woman replied with a big smile. She pats me on the arm and nods her head knowingly.

At three o'clock in the afternoon, I arrive at the albergue. I slip under the door at check-in. I will not worry if I have a place to stay for the night. At the next stop, Monte del Gozo, there are 800 beds. Why such a large number? All trails connect to Monte del Gozo before hiking into Santiago de Compostela. It is nice to know at the end there are more accommodations for hikers.

Seeing others here brings me joy and comfort. We talk about our events of the day.

"What is for dinner?" one of the guys shouts.

The women and I looked at each other. We burst into laughter. Since we are coming to the end of our journey, it would be nice to have a good dinner.

"We will prepare Italian pasta for everyone," our Italian couple yelled.

"I can help you in the kitchen," I suggested.

"No, thank you. We will prepare the meal, but you can clean up if you do not mind," the couple said.

"This is fine with me," I reply smiling.

"Men, let us go to the market to pick up what we need for our meal tonight," the cook said. We put our monies together and they dash to the market. While the men are out, the ladies begin to prepare the dining room for the dinner. I help to clean the table and chairs. The other women are in the kitchen cleaning the silverware.

"This is teamwork," I said with a smile.

"Yes, it is amazing how much less we need to do when many hands are helping," another friend chimed in.

After setting the dinner table, I take a step back to admire our shared efforts. "An actual sit down dinner tonight with beautiful folks is a joy," I proclaimed. The women and I hug mutually to appreciate one another for a good job well done.

Then I go to the showers to freshen up before dinner. I hear voices from the shower room. My friends are here.

"Hello. I am looking forward to eating a nice meal together tonight," I said.

"So am I," another friend agrees.

"It is so nice to make it this far and meet so many wonderful folks along the way," I said.

"I agree," a friend replied.

Now that I am ready, I go back to the dining room. After a moment or two, I heard the front door of the albergue open and shut.

"We are back," one of the guys said.

"Wonderful. Let me help you," I said. Taking a bag, I place it on the kitchen counter.

Rocky Bridge

"Now, let us begin our Italian cooking," the Italian chef of the evening announced proudly. We hear clattering of pots and pans as the cooks take them down from the shelves. I peek into the kitchen. The couple stares back at me.

"Could I help you with the salad?" I asked.

The couple looked at each other. "Okay. You may help only with the salad. That is all," they insisted. The couple speaks back and forth in Italian.

"I am in a kitchen with experts," I whispered to myself.

They cut up the fresh ingredients. Then pasta is dipped into hot boiling water. The sauce is simmering on the stove. Once the preparation is complete, the sauce is brought to the table. A big bowl of green salad large enough for everyone is also placed on the dinner table. We bless our meal and begin to share our feast. Pasta, sauce, and bread fill our plates. We drink both water and wine. We are quiet around the table as we take pleasure in eating.

"Three cheers for our cooks," I said delighted.

"Hooray, hooray, hooray," we said with appreciation.

"This is probably going to be our last meal together," a friend said.

"Yes, but we have each other for now. Let us enjoy this time together," another friend commented. Our cheers and toasts continue for a while. After the meal, we get up and hug each other.

"Tonight we are the magnificent seven. Buen Camino," we toasted in cheer and joy.

After a while, others join in our fun. The meal multiplies and feeds others. Good times with good friends makes this journey a moment to treasure for a lifetime. A friend plays his guitar and another plays his flute.

Hugs, fun, and cheers are shared among friends. I am grateful to stop here at Santa Irene for the night. The albergue is full, but folks passing through still stop to refresh themselves before they continue on the journey. Others will find a grassy area around the albergue where they sleep overnight.

Today started out on a rocky road, but in the end I shared a beautiful meal with wonderful friends. I am humbled and thankful.

Day 32 ~ Monte del Gozo

Joy

Leaving Santa Irene, I come to a fountain and refill my camelbak. Standing at the fountain, I cannot help but think that this time tomorrow I will be walking to Santiago de Compostela. The walk is quickly coming to an end. At the same time, this will be a new beginning for me.

Climbing the last hills of the Camino is before me today. I begin to walk nineteen kilometers to Monte del Gozo, which means Mount of Joy.

There is a saying; *all good things come to an end.* Indeed, it is for me. This walk has been one of the best things I have done in my life. I need to thank God for giving me the strength to have this adventure in my life and to live my dream. Without God's grace, I would not have come this far in the walk. I feel as if I have a new heart. Life is good.

I need to also thank God for my two amazing children which I love dearly. My children are my joy and hope for me to continue in life. The next generation is about to begin. My grandchildren are entering into my life. I will love them unconditionally as well. I have a new beginning and purpose now.

The fresh scents of the morning tickle my nose. I think the air is especially fresh this morning. I begin to sneeze and giggle. "This is funny. All this time I did not get sick on the walk. Today, I am sneezing. I hope I am not coming down with something. If I am going to be sick, it is okay," I chuckled.

Trekking through the hills, I notice the shade blocking out the sunlight. As I look up, I see tall eucalyptus trees. These trees have been here a long time. The large trunks and extreme height define their age. These trees support the hiker with shade. After a while, I walk into a tiny village called Rúa. This village clearly shows the direction to trek out of this area. I see folks in front of me making their way out of the village. Many of the nearby villages are beginning to look alike.

The cool air in the Galician region gives me strength to move along. After walking all this time, the coolness of the air especially helps at the end of the journey. My body is tired, but I am not dragging. The energy inside of me keeps me thriving.

As I make my way through woodlands and cross over highways, I hear the sound of an airplane. "Oh my, I think I am nearby Santiago de Compostela Airport, in

Lavacolla," I said with glee. The thought of an airport around the corner is simply incredible. I laughed with joy. As the sound becomes louder, I look up in the sky. Sure enough a metal bird is flying above me. I stop to gaze at it. "At least this bird will not have droppings like the blackbirds," I said laughing aloud.

Picking up my pace again, I see another vertical stone marker. I have K 12 until the finish line. Monte del Gozo is only about one or two hours from here. Walking on hard ground, I cross over another highway. In the distance, I see a large monument. As I approach the monument, there is an inscription saying "*Santiago.*"

"I cannot believe what I am seeing," I said delighted. My two hands hold my cheeks in awe. "This is real," I gasped. Below the sign, there is a carving of a large shell, a gourd, and a piece of rope twinned around it. I hug the stone marker. "I am getting closer to Santiago," I remarked. Without realizing it, I kiss the figure. Inside, I feel my emotions stirring up.

"Stop, stop, stop," I said quickly. "This does not need to happen here. I am not there yet. I need to walk further," I said calmly. Getting back on the trail, I venture on. I turned around and rapidly make my way back to the monument. I kissed it again.

"Hi, I am a pilgrim. It is nice to meet you," I said cheerfully. Hugging it again one final time, I let go.

I skip along the way until I realize I need to save my energy.

Markers are everywhere. Some are on poles and others are on vertical stone signs next to each other. This is helpful, especially for me. Sometimes I can easily get lost. Someway, somehow I find my way back. I guess this is how my life has been. Getting caught up in life only to forget what is important. Then there is a hand of compassion that guides me to return love. This time I will not stray away.

"My past is left behind here today. The Camino has made me realize this. My mistakes have been part of my humanness," I said softly.

Making a turn, I pass the tiny village of San Marcos. As I begin to climb a small hill, I see a large monument. "Pope John Paul II has visited here. This is amazing," I said.

Above the monument is a cross, a shell and a pilgrim. As I look to my side, I can see the little chapel of San Marcos. I stop in the chapel and sit in silence. After a while, I walk outside.

The last hill is Monte del Gozo. Standing on the mount, I see a glimpse of the cathedral towers of Santiago de Compostela. My feelings stir inside of me. I am kneeling on gravel between two monuments which look like pilgrims. The bronze statues stand at least fifteen feet high. One is a figure with a hat stretched out toward Santiago de Compostela. The statue is holding a bronze stick in the other hand. The other statue hails its hand out to the city with a staff in the other hand. These figures are pilgrims whose hands wave high toward Santiago de Compostela. Tears begin to flow down my face. I bow my head for a moment.

"Thank you, Lord. Without your grace, I would not be here. Tomorrow, I will be in Santiago de Compostela. This is a dream come true," I said with deep gratitude. Then I became silent. After a while, I came to my feet. I stuck out my hand like the monuments.

Arriving at the albergue, many rucksacks are already lined up outside of the door. I am not worried today. Securing a bunk tonight will not be difficult. As I place my rucksack at the end of the line, I make my way to the restroom. Washing my face restores my energy. The albergue will open in a couple of hours. I will go down the walkway to see if I can get something for dinner.

The layout of shops in this area gives a pilgrim an opportunity to pick up souvenirs before walking into the city. I visualize the hundreds of other folks making their final stop at the cathedral tomorrow. I hope to see some of my friends there. Seeing them again will be a joy before I make my way back to Germany. For now, I am happy to be here. At one of the shops, I meet some of my friends.

"Well tonight is our last night before the big day tomorrow," I said.

"Yes, we should have dinner together," a friend suggested.

We agree to share a meal tonight. Once again, we bought fruits, vegetables, and bread. Back at the albergue I find a bench to rest. Some of my friends sat with me. We chat for a bit. Then I experience *a eureka* moment.

Everyone is silent. I finally see the person I have heard about since I started this journey. Here he comes. He is blind and walking with his guide. Carrying a large rucksack on his back, a walking stick, and one hand on his guide, he makes his way from the top of the walkway to the albergue. With his hat behind his head resting on his rucksack and wearing sunglasses, he walks pass us. Both sides are filled with travelers looking at this amazing man trekking by.

Not a sound. Everyone is quiet. As he passes by me I begin to clap. Soon everyone joins in. The man smiles from ear to ear. It is as if he is thanking everyone. I sat in awe. The man and his guide stop and place their rucksacks down in line. This is a sight I will always remember.

The door to the albergue opens. I walk over to pick up my rucksack. Gradually, I make my way into the albergue to be processed in. I reach the counter and give my credential to the attendant.

Joy

"Do you have a passport?" he asked.

"Yes. Here it is," I replied.

"Where do you live?" he inquired.

"I live and work in Germany," I answered.

"Are you from Hawaii?" he asked.

"Yes, I am," I responded.

"Aloha and welcome," he said with a smile. He picks up his stamp. Then he looks at me, smiles, and stamps my credential.

"Thank you. Now I need to find a bunk for tonight." I said politely.

"You will not have a problem finding a bunk. There are many to choose from," the gentleman chuckled.

Standing at the entryway, all I could see are bunks after bunks and more bunks. "I am grateful to be here," I said. "This is wonderful. The last stop has a bunk for me tonight." I realize this is my last stop before Santiago de Compostela. I put my rucksack on my chosen bunk and go to the showers to freshen up.

Stepping outside of the albergue, I see my friends at a table. We share our food and relax until late afternoon. Someone begins to share his story about an event which he thinks is ridiculous. Another friend shares her story. We laugh about each other's adventures. Before we know it is time to go back to the albergue.

Once again, I reflect back upon this wonderful walk. Something brought me here to do this now rather than later. To wait until I retire from work would not have been the perfect timing. Now is the perfect time.

Not quite there yet, I feel full with zeal. When I first began this journey, I did not think I had the stamina to do this pilgrimage. Then I took one day at a time to build up my strength and overcome my fears. I think now it was not only to build up my strength, but my desire and determination to walk the Camino. All along I have yearned to do this walk. I now see things in a different light. I am a simple woman. This journey confirms my simplicity. I appreciate the simple things in life. Not having much is often more than I need. In my humility and my meekness, I am able to do impossible things, things that I would have never imagined I could do.

Later in the evening, I go back to San Marcos Chapel to attend Mass. There I connect with a friend from Poland.

"It is so nice to see you. How is your leg?" I asked.

"I am happy to see you as well. My leg is doing much better," she replied.

The priest overhears our conversation. He shares with us that he too will be a pilgrim for one week and that he is looking forward to his journey.

After Mass, I stare at Santiago de Compostela. Sunset is here. Different shades of pink, blue, and purple sweep across the city. It is a spectacular sight to see.

Joy

Tomorrow morning I will be in the city. Standing before the two monuments again I hug each one tightly. I sit down on the ground and lean my tired body against a statue. I rest my arms on my knees. There is no other place I would rather be than here this evening.

"I am only a stone's throw away to Santiago de Compostela," I whispered.

Day 33 ~ Santiago de Compostela

A New Heart

Today is a glorious day. I begin my last leg of my journey to Santiago de Compostela. At six o'clock in the morning, I leave Monte del Gozo. I walk slowly down the path. As the morning light breaks through to a new day, I feel energized.

Off to the side of a roadway, I see a sign in large letters that says: "*SANTIAGO.*" Below the sign is a large blue marker with a yellow shell. Shining my flashlight under the post, I illuminate the sign. Goose bumps are running up and down my arms. I stand with my walking stick in one hand, my flashlight in the other hand shining on the sign. My rucksack fits perfectly on me. I take a sip of water from my camelbak. I tiptoe forward and kiss the sign.

"I have waited thirty-three days for this special day. Words cannot begin to describe how I feel right now," I said in awe. Looking at the sign one last time, I take three deep breaths. Then I begin to trek the final four kilometers.

Reaching Porta do Camiño, I make my way through the city. I hear bells ringing from the cathedral. My heart is beating fast, but my feet are still going just one step at a time. I know there is no rush.

"I am here. Very soon I will be standing in front of the cathedral," I whispered. As I walk with other pilgrims through the winding streets, I keep silent. My silence is precious. "I am not in a hurry," I remind myself.

Then I walk through an archway. Next, I make a turn.

As I walk to the square, I face the front of El Obradoiro Façade; I gaze with awe, with joy, and with sweet tears running down my cheeks. I hold my hands to my mouth. I gasp at this breathtaking sight. Removing my rucksack, I fall to my knees and weep upon the cobblestone square.

"I give thanks and praise. I am here. The Camino is now mine. This is marvelous," I said silently through my tears. "Thank you God for bringing me here. Thank you for loving me and forgiving me," I cried. I do not want to move my body. I want to stay here. Then I feel a nudge from deep within me.

"Be still," a voice whispers.

"Yes," I said softly. Moving my rucksack behind me, I lean against it. I stare at the cathedral.

A New Heart

Looking up to the middle of the façade, I see a statue of Saint James standing high above overlooking the plaza. Today is perfect! The morning light twinkles on the old cathedral. The height is enormous. I have never seen anything like this. The towers are signs of strength rising high above the square. My eyes are fixed upon the towers. They are regal. Then as I lower my eyes, I see steps on both sides leading up to a stairway. The architectural design is superb.

On this journey, I have followed signs; walked over mountains; hiked through village after village; with the sun, the moon, the stars, the rain, and the wind on my face and on my back. The journey has brought me here. I have met many folks along the way. The adventures along the path have pointed me toward a new direction for my life. Washing away daily filth has cleansed me. I will not let my life be bleak. Living a life of love is now my desire.

I want to sit here and not do anything else today. Of course, this would be impossible. I need to go over to the Office of the Pilgrims to receive my Compostela. All the way from the office, down the stairs and into the street, folks are standing in line. As a pilgrim, I too get in line. I stand and patiently wait for my turn. As I make my way up the steps, excitement stirs inside of me. I see a hand waving. I go over to the counter and present my German and Spanish credentials.

"Ah, you have two credentials," the gentleman behind the counter said. He looked at all the different colored stamps.

"Yes, I do," I replied.

"Do you have a passport?" he asked.

"Here it is," I answered.

"Are you from Hawaii?" he inquired.

"I am from Hawaii, but I live and work in Germany," I replied.

Then he looked up at me and smiled. I see him beginning to write my name, **Dnam Lindam Christinam Magno** for Linda Christine Magno, August 23, 2007, on my Compostela. Tears stream down my face.

"These are tears of joy," I said to myself.

"Congratulations! Here is your Compostela," the man said with a big smile.

"Thank you," I said joyfully. I kiss it then press it lovingly against my chest.

At the bottom of the stairs, I meet some friends. We hold hands and dance in celebration. Hugging one another is wonderful and merry.

"We did it," we sang in glee.

I do an old ritual at the cathedral. I touch and walk around the columns of the Pórtico de la Gloria. Then I touch the statue of Mateo. He designed the Pórtico de la Gloria in the late eleventh century. Then I walk up a stairway behind the altar and embrace the bust of

Saint James. I did not want to let go. An outpouring of my tears flows generously, coming from deep within me. My hands become sweaty. In this very instant, I feel my pilgrimage has all been worthwhile.

While attending Mass in the Cathedral of Santiago de Compostela, I wonder to myself if any of my friends will be here. I immediately see my friends. Some of whom I thought had finished before me and that perhaps I would not see again. We embrace one another with heartfelt hugs. Seeing my friends from Spain, Hungary, Holland, Ireland, Austria, Italy and Poland bring tears of gladness.

I hope to see my friend from Italy. She helped me on the morning of the thunder and lightning when my flashlight went out. With a friend like her, I know there is hope. As I stand near a column facing the side altar, I feel a tap on my shoulder. Turning around, I see standing behind me my friend from Italy. We hug each other tightly.

"Thank you for saving me on that stormy morning," I whisper in her ear.

"We saved each other. Now we are here to celebrate our joy and accomplishment at this Mass," she said softly. More tears of happiness flow. We smile and kiss one another on one cheek and then the other cheek.

This completes everything. Having a chance to see my friends one last time makes this pilgrimage even more meaningful, for we have shared and helped one another all along this walk. I will remember the meals and stories we have shared together. When all is said and done, we simply gave support to one another to heal our soreness, our hurt, and our hearts. When we walked in the wrong direction, we guided one another with care.

Next to the cathedral is a five-star hotel. Way back when, this hotel was a hospital for pilgrims. Today, it is a fine hotel sitting on the same square as the cathedral. From a hospital to a hotel, it has continued a tradition. The hotel offers to the first ten pilgrims complimentary dining in one of the older parts of the hotel. It is a pilgrim's meal. As my friends and I make our way to stand in line, we discover we are the first.

"This is so special. I can barely believe we are the first in line," I said.

"Yes, this is a special reward," a friend remarked.

"Could someone please pinch me? I am in a dream," another friend replied.

"This is not a dream. We are the first ones," I answered.

As I turn around, I see the cathedral in plain view. It is wonderful. While I wait in line for dinner, I continue to fix my eyes upon the cathedral. At sunset, I see the lighting on the cathedral change from this morning. This morning the cathedral looked dark. Now it is a rich golden color. The façade and towers light up. There is not a cloud in the deep blue sky. It is clear. The cobblestone square is a reddish color. I can see the intricate architecture much better this evening. I am amazed.

"I need to pinch myself," I said delighted. Soon I hear footsteps coming in my direction. It is a hotel guard dressed handsomely in a suit. He is coming to escort us to dinner.

"Are you ready to have dinner in the hotel?" he asked.

"Yes, we are," we reply with great big smiles on our faces.

The guard escorted the ten of us into the hotel. Passing by the front lobby, I see people dressed elegantly. I absorbed the magnificence of this hotel. I feel some embarrassment that I am still dressed as a pilgrim. Meanwhile, my hunger pangs are erupting. My attire is not the best, but it will do for now. We are taken to a room reserved for pilgrims only. The hotel chef and staff have beautifully prepared our meals. The guard shows us where we can pick up our plates and return to the dining room. Water and wine are already set on our table.

After I get my meal from the buffet, I headed back to the dining room. I look at the pictures on the walls. They are of pilgrims from long ago making their way to Santiago de Compostela. As my friends walk into the room, we sit together. Others join us. At last, I pour my first glass of wine.

"Here is to all of us in this room and to all who have made the journey to Santiago de Compostela," I said in a toast. We all hold up our glasses.

"Cheers! Cheers! Cheers!" everyone shouts aloud, all in good spirits.

As I sip my wine, I savor it in my mouth. I slowly swallow it. My throat feels warm as the wine makes its way down.

"This is delicious. I waited until my last day to drink wine. It is worth every day of abstaining," I nodded.

The ambiance, the dinner, and the wine in this five-star hotel are a beautiful last supper. The food and wine are exquisite. Ending my journey like this is beyond my imagination.

The Camino has been a huge lesson in perseverance for me. Along the journey, I kept going even as I rid the fears in my life. Although I faced many difficulties, I did not give in. I did not quit. It would have been easy to complain and stop all together. Not I. Looking forward to the next day with a cheerful heart gave me the pleasure to continue the journey. I will not forget welcoming friends, their smiles, our laughter, our tears, and walking 500 miles.

In the beginning, I did not know what to expect on this pilgrimage. With a simple rucksack, a walking stick, a hat, a jacket, pants, and a pair of shoes I journeyed for thirty-three days. Along the way, I encountered pain and suffering. However, without pain and suffering I would not be celebrating today. At times along the journey, I experienced hurt and anger. Today, my tears are of joy and happiness.

I carried my life's baggage with me. This baggage contained dreams, happiness, sorrow, grief, pain, and hurt. My fears prevented me from letting go. I carried a heavy heart at times. As I trekked on my walk, my inner baggage became lighter and lighter. I let go. To lift my life's burdens, I realized I needed to reflect back in my life. The Camino has given me the grace to do just that. My life is now directed in a new way. Deep within me, I have created a new heart.

CPSIA information can be obtained at www.ICGtesting.com
Printed in the USA
BVOW032304060513

320055BV00001B/60/P